Date Due

KISSINGER'S ATLANTIC CHARTER

BY THE SAME AUTHOR

THOMAS HOBBES
SCIENCE AND METHOD OF POLITICS
PRINCIPLES OF POLITICS
SYSTEMATIC POLITICS
HISTORY OF THE POLITICAL PHILOSOPHERS
THE ANGLO-SAXON TRADITION
MAHATMA GANDHI
THE ATLANTIC COMMUNITY
THE GRANDEUR OF ENGLAND AND THE ATLANTIC COMMUNITY
THE ATLANTIC COMMONWEALTH
FOR GOD'S SAKE, GO!

KISSINGER'S
ATLANTIC CHARTER

by

Sir George Catlin

COLIN SMYTHE
GERRARDS CROSS 1974

First published in 1974 by Colin Smythe Ltd.,
Gerrards Cross, Buckinghamshire

ISBN cloth   0 901072 06 0

ISBN paperback 0 901072 07 9

Produced in Great Britain
by the Van Duren Press, Gerrards Cross, Bucks.

To
HENRY A. KISSINGER
Nobel Peace Prizewinner and Secretary of State
continuator
of the policy of
President Dwight D. Eisenhower

PREFACE

THE FIRST chapter of this book does not pretend to do more than provide a factual background to an argument at once contemporary and yet perhaps the most vital for peace in this century, namely the relation of the countries of Western Europe, especially of France and Germany, with each other, and of this western portion of Europe as a whole with the wider Atlantic Community and with the Soviet Union and Far East. Some aspects of these issues I earlier discussed in my *Anglo-Saxon Tradition* (1939), as a study of like-mindedness in values on the verge of the Second World War, and in my *Atlantic Community* (1959).

It is at this present time, named, happily or not, the "year of Europe", that we approach what can very properly be called "the Fork in the Road" between the Atlantic emphasis and the North West European emphasis, where it chances that especially Britain (although not Mr. Edward Heath) stands poised.

I would wish to call attention to Dean Eugene Rostow's recent book, *Peace in the Balance,* and to express my indebtedness to Professor Alastair Buchan's Russell C. Leffingwell Lectures, *Power and Equilibrium in the 1970s,* just published and which I had the fortune to see before hurrying this book to press.

5 Wilton Place,
London, S.W.1.

GEORGE CATLIN
14th August, 1973.

ERRATA & ADDENDA

p.12, line 16, read "yet not a recognized equilibrium".

p.21, lines 8-10, "On my suggestion to its chairman, the Pilgrims invited him to London to elaborate his position: and this Dr. Kissinger did on 12 December 1973."

p.37, between lines 36 and 37, insert the top two lines from the following page together with missing words so that the passage reads, "Again the credibility of Edward Heath is eroded, as was recently that of Presidents Johnson and Nixon."

"After joining the Common Market Six, our export over import failure."

p.46, line 3, read "our local ex-Prime Minister".

p.85, line 6, read "could by Executive fiat".

p.96, line 12, read "Maybe the sooner Mr. Kissinger was out of the".

p.119, line 31, "principles this year (1973)." '

Contents

I

From Bryce to Kissinger

TALK about crisis grows wearisome. It is, nevertheless, my conviction that, if the momentum of this century, after two World Wars, towards internationalism is lost—the widest practical internationalism that is realistic—then the process will begin again which some of us have seen twice in our lifetime.

Wars do not occur overnight. When diplomacy, perhaps tentative, exploratory adventures with their own touch of genius, breaks down, when a mutual confidence (which is prepared to take military risks) fades, itself probably sustained by long historical experience, then bit by bit the war-machine begins to be put into order, with its cast-iron military schedules, its military-industrial complex, its subsidiary schedules, its well-placed orders for *materiel*. Once geared, it is politically difficult to dismantle. Jealousy, rivalry, ambition, national interest, a limited national patriotism, moral fury, all support it. That States, and not only England and Scotland or the Thirteen Colonies, actually unite is dismissed as irrelevant. The quadrille of rival powers, the true dance of death, begins to take shape. Maybe, as Lloyd George said of World War I, the machine is "backed over the precipice"; maybe, as Winston Churchill said of World War II, it was all unnecessary and with better, more intelligent statesmanship it need not have occurred. The fact is it did occur—and will. Granted the will, the pretext, the emotions, indeed the propaganda, ideals are never lacking.

Whatever the type of society which men have sought after, the problem has been one of acquiring the means for its effective achievement. The systematic study of politics hence becomes a study of ends but, not less, also of effective means and a study of power. Sometimes that power and control are acquired by co-operation (a point which Hobbes overlooked) and sometimes only by domination.

In the days of the Roman Empire there was no issue (except perhaps in the Euphrates valley) of a balance of power. Rome held the power. There was a *pax romana*, even if it was sometimes achieved by *"laying waste"*. However, with the break-up of the Roman Empire and indeed of the Carolingian Empire, and from the rivalries of the barbarians, there emerged in the West two major *foci* of power: that of the Germanic people and of the so-called Holy Roman Empire, described by Voltaire as "neither Holy nor Roman nor an Empire", but still in the days of the Emperors, from Frederick Barbarossa and earlier to the Emperor Charles V and later, an effective force, and that of the Gallic people, slowly crystallizing as "France", not of the weak Counts of Paris and of the Isle de France but, at the beginning of the modern period, as the centralized France of Richelieu.

The political picture was not of an authoritative peace enforced, as under the earlier Empire, "by arms and laws", but of a balance between Bourbon and Hapsburg which was yet not recognized equilibrium nor a stable Concert of Europe. Even against the Moslem Turk France was sometime found on the other side.

When the direct rule of the Plantaganets, affirmed at Agincourt, faded away, for England a new policy began with Wolsey. It is on the historic record that to this day the Queen of England is titular "Duke (*sic*) of Normandy". It is likewise on the record that it was the University of Paris that supported the Plantagenets against Jeanne d'Arc. The new policy was to be one, not usually of direct involvement in the land army struggles of Europe, but one of support, usually financial, of those in Europe who resisted domination by any one Power, simultaneously maintaining English pre-eminence at sea.

The maritime rivalry with Spain, also looking across the Atlantic, was explicit, for a while, but the land balance of power in Continental Europe was maintained, first at Blenheim and Waterloo against French predominance and then, no less, against the Kaiserdom and a Hitler who had decided to reverse his own earlier judgment given in *Mein Kampf* and to fight on two fronts. Resistance to any one Power dominating Western Europe (or even too blatantly Eastern Europe) was central to British foreign policy. Conversely the Franco-Russian agreement at Tilsit was consonant with French policy, and Napoleon's Retreat from Moscow a catastrophe for it.

It was the eighteenth century policy of Chatham to contain French continental ambitions in Europe on the heights of Quebec as on the plains of India. It was continued by Pitt the Younger against Napoleon's policy of uniting all Western Europe under himself as Emperor. It gave no spiritual satisfaction to Jefferson to find himself, in resisting what Americans held to be the illegal and immoral British doctrine of right of search on the open seas, "objectively" in the same camp as the Corsican, whose uncompleted work, a century later, Adolf Hitler endeavoured to perfect in military enterprises speedier and no less brilliant than his own.

For a century the Western hemisphere, Spanish, British and, in more limited fashion, French or Portuguese, was to remain colonial, agricultural, self-isolated and transport-isolated, of minor weight—perhaps less in the case of Spain— in the counsels of the Great Powers which, ignoring Asia, were almost entirely European and so remained until the Russian collapse at Port Arthur. It was then that the pre-dominance of Europe, at least in its own eyes, over the entire historical and cultural scene, begun at Marathon, went into eclipse. There had indeed been glimpses of another world in the days of Marco Polo, who yet merely aroused incredulity. Now Europe went into eclipse, except for the revived Russian super-power; Asia and North Africa emerged again—"the Greeks are children" had said the Egyptians—and America also.

Already de Tocqueville, in the days of Andrew Jackson, was calling attention to the significance of the "great American experiment", not so much democratic as representative in government, and Lincoln, following Jefferson, was giving a new importance to democracy. The period of the Civil War, but also that of "gun-boat" Palmerston (a Liberal), ameliorated by the tact of the Prince Consort, Albert, was one of uneasy tension between what Mr. Secretary George Marshall, in my presence, called "the mother country" and the emerging grown-up daughter, a tension which lasted during certain South American boundary disputes affecting Venezuela.

A new period begins with the Presidency of Theodore Roosevelt and with that influential time when James Bryce was British Ambasasdor in Washington. Just as the portrait of the relevant British Secretary for Foreign Affairs appears in the corridor of the American Embassy in London in connection with the settlement of the Oregon boundaries, so the bust of Lord Bryce is to be found by the curious most honourably placed in a niche of the waiting room of the American Senate in the Capitol, Washington. The United States, growing ever more nationally adult and confident, was beginning to throw off its inferiority feeling and its resentment of a past colonial status, and this has not yet fully occurred in Canada. It began to recall, not least in the Commonwealths of Virginia, Massachusetts, Pennsylvania and Kentucky, the finer record of the colonial period. Eccentric Scottish millionaires such as Andrew Carnegie, flying the two national flags sewn together when host to Edward VII, celebrated the new outlook; and Welsh-speaking miners continued to fill the mining towns of Pennsylvania and later, in time of war, were addressed in Welsh by a British Minister, Jim Griffiths.

The ideas of Evelyn Wrench, of the English-speaking Union, today under a cloud deliberately contrived by *enragés* Europeans, became significant. One of the most ardent advocates of the closest Anglo-American relations, the naval historian, Admiral Mahan, was very nearly appointed to a chair in Oxford (dislike of innovation prevailed), Theodore Roosevelt and A. J. Balfour had under discussion a formal memorandum, described by me in earlier books, which contemplated remarkable steps of political unification*.

The relationship seemed encouraging indeed for future United States-Commonwealth relations, although the most striking tribute, all sentiment apart, to the political and strategic importance of this is to be found in, of all places, the testimony of Adolf Hitler, in *Mein Kampf*, pointing out to Germans that these two countries must always be treated in diplomacy as fundamentally parts of one political entity, in so many aspects like-minded, whatever the difference at the competitive level, not of high politics, but of low commerce. Here indeed the philosophy of Edmund Burke, rising above the cleverness of brisk anti-patriotic journalism, seemed to apply:

"In the intercourse between nations we are apt to rely too much on the instrumental part . . . men are not tied to one another by paper and seals. They are led to associate by resemblances, by uniformities, by sympathies. It is with nations as with individuals. Nothing is so strong a tie of amity between nation and nation as correspondence in laws, customs, manners, and habits of

* *Vide* my *Atlantic Community* (1959); *The Grandeur of England and the Atlantic Community* (1966); *The Atlantic Commonwealth* (1969).

life . . . The secret, unseen but irrefragable, bond of habitual intercourse holds them together."

The historic tendency of the Democrat Party, whether led by Woodrow Wilson in the First World War or by Franklin Delano Roosevelt in the Second, has been to adopt a global or universalist outlook. The United States has prudently declined to tie its hands by particular privileged relationships, continental or racial, preferring to give its support to world organisations such as the League of Nations or the United Nations. Indeed the Democrats in the end were advocating the involvement, or were already involving the country, in more wide-spread obligations, at least on paper through the League and the U.N., than the Republicans who, during the time of Mr. Secretary Kellogg, tended to place their confidence in the rule of law, international Courts of Justice and declarations against war in any national interest or, as in the later days of John Foster Dulles, in numerous alliances, with the accompanying commitments, of which NATO was only one. Nevertheless the "Truman Doctrine" as it applied to the Eastern Mediterranean and the numerous defence organizations "East of Suez" to which the United States gave its name, after negotiation by Mr. Dulles, were not dissimilar in their "containment" policy.

In this diplomatic network of world-wide extent there were yet some relationships of a regional character which constituted a special interest, maybe with Latin America and today with Japan. France, for reasons more closely related to French antagonism to British policy than to any enthusiasm of the Bourbon monarchy for the new republic, to this day claims a special relationship. Of all these, for reasons historical and ethnic, and thanks to the proximity of the Republic and the Commonwealth in North America (although maybe the Canadians are never so "loyal" as when tweaking the American tail), the Anglo-American special relationship is the best established. As President Truman said to me in 1964, in Independence, Missouri, in repudiating the substitution for 'special" of such tepid phrases as "natural and historical": "It exists, doesn't it?" Indeed it may exist in a form which gives some displeasure to those in France who are described as "European Europeans", who view without pleasure what Hitler recognized as the traditional inter-relation of *les pouvoirs anglosaxons*—a displeasure re-enforced by jealousy, cultural snobbery and what Bentham would have described as malignant private interests; and

15

resentment comparable to that of Austria once against Germany.

The problem has, in this century, not been one of lack of American interest in closer international relations. The entire record of Woodrow Wilson (although here balanced by his stress on "self-determination") is to the contrary. The issue during the Second World War, and during the time immediately preceding it, was rather the form these relations were to take: whether primarily relying upon the moral authority of "the Rule of Law", public opinion, and international tribunals, or on (at least in principle) world-wide institutional structures, such as the League of Nations or the United Nations.

The first of these, the League, collapsed under the stress of making an executive decision with the oncoming of World War II, the tepid support and uncommitted attitude of the U.S. Senate, and the active hostility, since the Finnish wars, of the U.S.S.R. The project for the second, although with very limited executive power (instead of the original Taft plan of "maintaining peace") and with the U.S. Senate appeased by being assured of a right of veto, was supported so vigorously by Franklin Roosevelt that alternatives of a more regional or more firmly executive nature were thrust into the background. What emerged was "a forum of debate", unkindly described by Winston Churchill as "jaw-jaw, better than war-war".

These alternatives, however, were far from negligible. Some had concentrated upon international organization for specific functions, such as the postal services. Others—and these, it is important to note, British or American in origin —sought, as did Lionel Curtis, a close political integration or, as in the influential *Union Now* of Clarence Streit, a constitutional federal union on the analogy of the original plan of the American Founding Fathers. Later, in war-time and after, while some became emphatically universalist, not regionalist, Clarence Streit published his *Union Now with Britain*. The writings at this time of scholars such as Brebner, writing on Anglo-American-Canadian relations—the Trilateral—merit attention. Meanwhile federal unionist resolutions were not only discussed but received the formal support of several American State legislatures, and indeed a resolution of the same intent but of a more dilute character was carried in the U.S. Senate by Senator Ball of Minnesota. Eminent names, like those of Mr. Justice Roberts, Under-

Secretary William Clayton and, later, Senator Estes Kefauver, of Tennessee, Mr. Secretary Christian Herter and indeed, in the Eisenhower days, Vice President Richard Nixon, were added to the supporting list. As late as 1973 a resolution in favour of an international convention in support was passed *nem. con.* by the Senate but failed to pass the House committee.

One problem with the federal union proposals connected with the name of Clarence Streit was that they visualized a written constitution, and the federal character of the proposals acquired an almost ideological importance. For this very reason they were less than acceptable in the official policy, for example, of France and Britain, and were explicitly repudiated by such a spokesman for the European movement as Mr. Duncan Sandys. Mr. Edward Heath stated that he himself had never used the phrase "United States of Europe". However, this objection to a constitutional legalism, in advance of its time, of the Federal Union movement, regional or universal, did not apply to the Atlantic Union movement, which was committed to no specific stand, *pro* or *con,* on the federal issue.

Actually the war-time alliance of Britain, Canada and America took robust post-war shape in the framework of the Atlantic Treaty Alliance, with its later ex-enemy adjuncts, and in the specific defence (but also, under its charter, civilian) organization of NATO and similar treaty organizations in the East. That, beyond mere defence, this should increasingly assume a political form was the proposal of the Atlantic Union Movement. According to Wilcox and Haviland, Streit, Walter Lippmann and myself were the first to put the concept of the Atlantic Community into circulation in the late 'Thirties. We were the first Atlantic citizens. Certainly the demand for "organic consultation", i.e. international consultation on policy at all levels, down to the departmental, and this as a routine, and not as an exceptional or merely mechanical, matter, was urged by myself and so advocated by Walter Lippmann, as "War Aim One", in his *U.S. War Aims.*

It has now entered into the ordinary parlance of diplomacy with some significant measure of acceptance. The Republican Presidential Candidate in 1940, Wendell Willkie, whose foreign affairs adviser I temporarily became, went further, to the point of advocating common American-British Commonwealth citizenship—a proposal not so extravagant in view of Churchill's offer of a common Anglo-French citizenship.

Many of those who viewed with disapproval the comedy of a "49th" or "51st" State(all Canada becoming the 52nd?) smartly changed their coats when the issue was that of Britain becoming a "Ninth State" of Continental Europe. However, the European Union movement sprang from quite different roots (although not from dissimilar ideas, in contrast with the earlier nationalistic and sovereign legal approach) from those of the American war-time and post-war unionism, And here, in an important sense, the Atlantic concept had chronological priority.

The European Union Movement, in its practical importance, was a post-World War II development. Apart from arguments about the requirements of lasting peace which, as with Dante, looked back to the Roman Empire or to Charlemagne and the Holy Roman Empire, literary advocacy of a united Europe, as distinct alike from the nationalism which expressed itself with Danton and the imperialism of Napoleon, goes back to Victor Hugo. Specific advocacy, in organizational form, one finds in the PanEuropa organization of Count Coudenhove-Kalergi, the Austrian diplomat (and himself, surprisingly, part Japanese). More successful, because less specifically limited in scope, was the advocacy of Jean Monnet, initially not a friend of British entry into Europe.

In this movement there was from the beginning a conflict of interpretations between "federalists" and "functionalists", the latter with the more modest ambition of setting up "Sovereign High Authorities" (to which ambassadors could be accredited), providing international control in specific activities such as the marketing of coal and steel.

However, as early as the late 'Forties, leading figures such as M. Robert Schuman, Foreign Minister and Prime Minister of France, emphasized that, in the end, a political integration would be inevitable since at some point the functional authorities would require instruction from some central authority, itself sovereign. The project for a European Defence Community, more ambitious than the localized functional authorities, limited to coal and steel and the peaceful uses of atomic energy, collapsed in the days of M. Mendès-France and Sir Anthony Eden, largely due to British lack of enthusiasm. Even when British policy in Europe changed (from a specific calculation of propaganda advantage), only the economic advantages of union, in the form of the

European Economic Community (which could itself be advocated as functional), were stressed. The awkward question of political integration, whether "federal union" or *union des patries,* or however it was ultimately to be handled, in the European Commission in Brussels, was left for future evolution to decide, without forcing contemporary politicians into unpopular commitments. However, if feasible, a unified foreign policy was contemplated, although what this would spell, e.g. in terms of the Middle East, to this day remains obscure. This EEC or Common Market development, in intention more than a Customs Union, following the Hague Conference and the Strasburg European Assembly, was pioneered by various voluntary bodies of the late 'Forties, pre-eminently the *Nouvelles Equipes* which had the distinction of being composed of actual party political delegations. It is significant to add that these were in most cases of a predominantly Catholic confessional character. That of the MRP of France was led by M. Robert Schuman and M. Maurice Schumann, that of Western Germany by Dr. Konrad Adenauer, and that of Italy by Signor Alcide de Gasperi. The small multi-party and multi-confessional British delegation, in the absence of the Duchess of Atholl, was at the Luxemburg Conference of 1948 led by myself as a member of the *Nouvelles Equipes* International Executive Committee. This Committee, which lost importance with the second coming to power of M. de Gaulle, was assuredly not anti-American nor anti-Atlantic, while indeed being anxious to cultivate British support.

The early European movement, while sustained by certain principles (not least in terms of European and even Carolingian identity, following what was felt to be in certain essentials a distinctively European civil war), and certainly concerned to restore the damaged prestige of France and to bring Germany and Italy back into the Concert of Europe, was primarily economic and indeed deliberately so. During the war these countries were "objectively" on the wrong side of the firing line. Unlike the discussion of American-British-Canadian relations, the union of Germany, France, Italy in 1939-44 was an affair of the Third Reich, and discussion of support for it out of the question for the Allies. Subsequently there could be discussion indeed, but Bonn, Rome and even Paris still remained peripheral. In my own book of 1959, *The Atlantic Community,* these centres were conscious additions to what I said in an earlier (1940) study of Anglo-

American relations. In 1965 Mr. Drew Middleton provided a survey of the whole situation. The Atlantic field of interest was primarily that of defence, and so later continued in the shape of NATO, although a focal rallying point of principle was to be found in the Atlantic Charter, signed by Roosevelt and Churchill in Placentia Bay, Newfoundland, and hence of no small symbolic importance.

As in the case of the earlier federal v. functional issue, so it became increasingly apparent that there was an Atlantic Community issue, originating in considerations of common defence, over against a European Community issue, also by implication political but developed in terms of economic considerations and a common market. With many members common to both, it was all too easily assumed that there was no conflict between the two—and it was indeed most true that there was no *necessary* conflict, provided no one began to search for what was called "an identity" which would exclude the other—no longer a matter of America, Britain and Canada against Germany, Italy and Vichy France, but of Continental Europe and Britain against America and, maybe, Canada. If Western Europe was, however, no longer to be regarded as, institutionally, a recent pioneering member within the wider Atlantic community, but as a self-conscious political entity on its own, over against others, then clearly problems, still unsolved to this day, arose. It is these problems which are the concern of the present book.

Against various exclusive European Movements in, for example, Britain, an Atlantic Unity (or Union) Council has been shaped. In a conscious endeavour to provide a formula, acceptable alike to those who concentrate on the importance of EEC and those who insist that the European policies must, to be acceptable, be shaped within the wider Atlantic framework and field of consultation, a statement of aims has been made.

"The purpose of the Council is to propagate support for the Atlantic Community, subscribing to the principles of the Atlantic Charter and opposed to any policies which will in effect produce discord, rivalry and schism between the partners in the Atlantic Treaty organisation. It is within this Atlantic framework that it finds its identity and that, as internationalist, it gives support to EEC and to like Western European democratic institutions as components of a larger Atlantic partnership. The positive road to world peace is held to be found in the integration of the widest areas practicable."

Dr. Henry Kissinger has, very logically from his own point of view, gone back to the first Atlantic Charter for his proposed re-statement of the principles of co-operation. It may be that these will be sufficiently explicit for those who in fact do not agree with them to make this divergence clear. On my suggestion to its chairman, the Pilgrims have invited him to London to elaborate his position; and this Dr. Kissinger is expected to do in October of this year.

II

Atlanticism: The Present

PRIOR to and during the earlier years of the First World War the discussion of international organization for peace had largely been in terms of World Courts or tribunals, reinforcing international laws. Even the Czar had given his support to the Hague Court, although a suspicion that Russian artillery might be inferior to Austrian had perhaps supplied a reinforcing motive. Imperialism, in Britain and France, might be regarded with increasing suspicion in liberal quarters, and the notion of appeal to arbitration might spread, but the notion of absolute national sovereignty and *salus populi*, except when carried by the Kaiser, against treaty obligations, to what were regarded as indecent logical extremes, remained unimpaired.

Towards the end, however, of the pre-Second World War period, discussion gained momentum favouring a union of States going beyond that "free union of sovereign States" which was the formula of the League of Nations and, indeed, in some cases reflected the union of the erstwhile colonies in the constitution of the United States. There could be a sovereign union of free States. In some cases, as was said in the last chapter, this could be a constitutional federal union; in others the advocacy of a practical habit of institutionalized collaboration, rather on a Commonwealth model and even down to the departmental level, not excluding in particular functional cases a full integration.

These proposals were, as already said, primarily North American in initiative, although the early work of Lionel Curtis and, in Europe, of Coudenhove-Kalergi, cannot be overlooked. What is here noteworthy is that Atlantic Union proposals, not least those of Clarence Streit, are not a late afterthought to European Union proposals. *Atlantic Union as the earlier and indeed the original programme, preceded European and European-British union plans.* If Atlantic Union plans have not developed equally fully and speedily, the blame must in some measure lie with the U.S. Senate, despite its support *nem. con.* (but perhaps not to be taken too seriously) for a federal union delegate world conference. Expression was found in the Atlantic Charter declaration, the Atlantic Treaty and alliance, in NATO and, on a different, academic, but not insignificant level, in the Atlantic Institute. But concentrated energy, until Dr. Henry Kissinger's recent proposals, was focused first upon the popular global idealism of the United Nations (1942-52), which energy then was diverted (1952-72) to attention to South East Asia, with the United States being invited to expend its energies chiefly in becoming a Pacific Ocean Power, with Japan an auxiliary. Specifically "Atlantic", as distinct from "European", proposals have been increasingly side-tracked. Emergence from this diplomatic confusion and distortion is a matter of only the other day.

Hence discussion for the last two and a half decades, and pre-eminently during the last decade, has been not in Atlantic terms, except in the very marginal interpretation given to these by General George C. Marshall and by M. Robert Schuman and others, but in European terms, whether, as with de Gaulle, almost exclusively Continental or, as in the case of Edward Heath, with Britain (as distinct from the British Commonwealth) included as intrinsic. To the perspectives of British politics, regarded not least in the United States as a key to the success of the entire operation, and to policy elsewhere, related thereto, we must now turn.

The present problem of Atlanticism, which by 1975 may reach what has been called, at high levels of strategic expertise, a "fork in the road", is that of its relation with European Continentalism and, specifically, with that part of Europe which lies in the West, outside the Communist bloc and north of the Pyrenees.

In post-war Britain, Conservative governmental policy on the issue of joining the Common Market (EEC) or, as it was rather misleadingly called, "Entry into Europe", underwent four phases.

The first was that of post-war reconstruction and the primarily Churchillian phase, which was one of emphatic benevolence but scarcely more (expressed in Churchill's Zurich speech of September, 1946), towards the whole policy of unification of Western Europe (not, however, including the historic Iberian Peninsula or the European area of the old Eastern Roman Empire), the old Franco-German feuds being now considered at an end. This, however, fell short of the commitment of Britain to the Continent, despite particular guarantees of alliance such as Ernest Bevin gave to France against any possible *revanchiste* Germany. The foreign policy of Winston Churchill and of Ernest Bevin was not discontinuous and certainly emphasised the British "identity" and role. Active although Winston Churchill, out of office and unemployed, was in the Strasburg European Parliament, in his own eyes his Zurich speech was almost certainly less important and more "diplomatic" than those which he had given in Fulton, Missouri, in March, 1946, and before the Virginia Legislature*.

In this phase, so far as Britain was concerned, there were two ambiguities. On the one hand, although Churchill himself at Strasburg might play the role of "the Great Commoner", urging the claims of the European Assembly against the nationally based Council of Ministers, he was not until 1953 Prime Minister again and able to state Government policy. He could also claim an *alibi* in Europe even when Prime Minister, complaining that the Conservative Party machine "was too strong for me". His Party rather shared the views of Anthony Eden (incidentally listed as a supporter of "Atlantic Union"), shown when Eden declared that he "was not a European animal". Churchill could also claim an *alibi* as regards Europe in terms of the Anglo-American "special interest" implications, emphasised in his Fulton speech—a phrase later reiterated to me, in Independence, Missouri, by President Truman and affirmed by President Nixon—but one which sticks in some throats, particularly in the French throat.

The ambiguity between the Fulton position, which stressed the alignment, historically and in two wars, of Britain and North America, and Churchill's new Zurich "Concert of Europe" position, continued—although an ambiguity it was thought undesirable to emphasize in those days. The major European leaders, not least those of the French M.R.P., were, at that early time, assiduous (as I personally discovered as a member of the international executive committee of the

* *Vide* the author's Winston Churchill Memorial Lecture, *Atlanticism*, Westminster College, Fulton, Mo., 1969, and also his *For God's Sake, Go*, Colin Smythe, 1972 (henceforth referred to as *For God's Sake*). Earlier and relevant books are his *Anglo-Saxon Tradition* (1939), *The Atlantic Community* (1959), *The Grandeur of England and the Atlantic Community* (1966) and *The Atlantic Commonwealth* (1969).

Nouvelles Equipes, of which the M.R.P. was a member) in polite emphasis on their loyalty to NATO and Atlanticism —even not hesitating to compare French relations with *la France d'Outremer* and the Gabon republic with those of England with Canada, Australia and New Zealand. The underlying ambiguity or ambivalence became obscured by publicists who wished to attach Churchill's name exclusively to Zurich, with Fulton forgotten, or by politicians who had their personal axe to grind. Indeed few were more *enragés* Europeanizers without reservation than the London *Sunday Times* which, by a political quirk, was, marvellous to say, owned by Lord Thomson, a Canadian.

It is a far cry from Churchill to the position of 1972 when, under criticism from EEC Ministers, Foreign Secretary Sir Alec Douglas-Home had, as reported in the Press, to disclaim the view that "one must not do anything to annoy the United States". Maybe there is indeed a time for annoyance and a time for mutual confidence. For myself, perhaps I may be permitted to say that here I am entirely Churchillian, supporting the American and the Atlantic cause on the assumption that I know what these are. This balanced policy requires a restatement today, thirty years on.

The second, "Eden", phase of Conservative policy was that of the scepticism of Foreign Office experts, as distinct from idealist amateurs, as to whether any scheme so pretentious as that for the unification of Western Europe (including, at this stage, Defence) and going well beyond both Benelux and also Coal and Steel functional proposals, was "realistic" or would ever "get off the ground" or, for contemporary purposes, radically change the traditional structure of politics and diplomacy. A diffused benevolence on principle towards fraternity, world peace and European unity was routine; but the United Nations organization, largely composed of Arabs and Asians, already involved quite enough expenditure of money and energy on idealistic blue-prints for Utopia. An ending of the immemorial Franco-German feud, symbolized by a joint Mass in Notre Dame, was indeed desirable and might be practicable—a European Union with no aggressive Napoleonic or Hitlerite intentions—and the Benelux Union an interesting pioneer Association. It was not yet seen as a British or American plan—one of *les pouvoirs anglosaxons*—but as a matter for French and German diplomacy in dealing with ex-enemies and the legacy of Vichy. The new experiment (1952) of the Coal and Steel "Sovereign High Author-

25

ity", with its own ambassadors accredited to it, although evoking only the most cautious enthusiasm, seemed to involve no excessive commitment. The need for effective military defence and security, underlined by Russian policy in Prague since the death of Masaryk, and again in Hungary, and the patent inability of the disillusioning and impotent U.N. to provide this security, pushed forward acceptance of the North Atlantic Treaty (14th April, 1949)—advocated in the previous year in the United Nations by Louis St. Laurent, Premier of Canada—and later on (Lisbon, 1949) of that implementing organisation called NATO.

However, the Messina Conference and the ensuing Rome Treaty of March, 1957, were given realistically a diplomatic cold shoulder. Earlier (1954) M. Mendès-France, as Prime Minister of France, had brought French military policy into accord with that of Anthony Eden by side-tracking the European Defence Community proposals. Later on, with de Gaulle in charge in France, the Rome Treaty was dealt with in a more subtle fashion. The French President first signed the Treaty but then gave it an anti-federalist inter-pretation, which threw a new light on what "commitment by treaty" could involve—an interpretation sharply different from that of the European Founding Fathers, including Robert Schuman and Maurice Schumann among the French.

To the surprise of the British Foreign Office, in the days of Harold Macmillan, who succeeded Eden, the Common Market arrangements issuing from the Treaty showed clear signs of producing concrete results, especially economic, which in this area of realistic diplomacy were likely to impinge more specifically on British interests than had been anticipated.

Hence, in the third phase under Macmillan, defensive economic action was taken through a regional free trade area of seven countries, largely North European in character, and with Britain the largest partner, in the shape of the European Free Trade Area (EFTA, 1960). Harold Mac-millan's agent for this construction was Reginald Maudling, President of the Board of Trade and later Chancellor of the Exchequer. This newer Europe was soon at sixes and sevens. The economic result was half-hearted, beneficial but not spectacular. Above all it did not provide that wider market for commerce which the more enterprising business men, property developers and so on, but also the more vulnerable and emerging British industries, supported by British banks, were beginning to demand with urgency.

Following the earlier enthusiasm of 1945 for the United Nations, and short of non-regional world free trade on a GATT basis, the NAFTA or AFTA (Atlantic Free Trade Area) plan, supplied at least in blue-print the largest market of all—one of about 450 million people, including North America, Western Europe and Australasia. But the wind at that time was not blowing in this direction, not least owing to the indifference or South-East Asian preoccupation of the majority of the U.S. Senate, which must bear a large measure of the blame. President Eisenhower certainly did not lack interest in Atlantic proposals, NATO among them, nor did his successor, President John F. Kennedy. During all this era the U.S. Presidency emerges more creditably than Congress, although the work of particular war-time Senators and Congressmen, such as Senators William Ball and Estes Kefauver, are not to be forgotten.

Likewise the world-scattered British Commonwealth—although strategically distributed half-moon-wise around the United States, centre-piece of its jig-saw—in spite of its political grandeur, did not offer the market the business men demanded. Despite Canadian Lord Beaverbrook's earlier efforts, it did not present itself, unless tariff-integrated with the United States, as fully economically viable. Canada played a different and more nationalist game, with the United Nations as its internationalist fig-leaf. (Later, as with Belgium, nationalism, once let loose from Pandora's box, was to become a nemesis for Canada.)

Nor did the world of business share the confident statesmanship of de Gaulle, who did so much to raise the stature of France and who held that these business negotiations were mere "affairs of the *bourse*". They were what Edmund Burke, also considering politics as the mistress of economics, had described earlier as matters of "pepper and calico"—modern journalists will add "kangaroo tails"—"and other such low concerns". De Gaulle may have been perverse but at least he belonged to a heroic epoch, the return of which is required so much today.

Hence a fourth phase. EFTA, not being the kind of stuff to raise the emotions of the electorate and a General Election pending which the government was not certain that it would win, other approaches had to be considered and re-considered. That voiced by Churchill at Zurich offered a

basis—admittedly it was but one of Churchill's two bases—
and could be made more precise and binding. The sometime
Tory Party Whip (1955-59) and Lord Privy Seal (1960-63),
Edward Heath, was, in this case, chosen by Macmillan as his
negotiator—de Gaulle is alleged to have remarked, "and
then we shall only have Heath to deal with"—and, desiring
a niche in history, became personally identified with the new
policy. Far from being cool towards the new European Common Market, Mr. Heath was enthusiastic for British Entry as
the recipe for a better future for Britain, if not exactly for
the Commonwealth.

As M. Pompidou much later remarked, in January, 1973,
with more warmth than tact: "I sometimes thought that
Heath was the only Englishman favourable to the entry of
Britain into the Common Market." There was a paucity of
enthusiasm. Unfortunately this new Macmillan policy was on
a collision course with the policy for Europe, Paris-orientated
and carefully planned, which the President of France, M. de
Gaulle, at that date wanted. The consequence was, in 1963,
what Harold Macmillan called "the brutal slamming of the
door". The question at issue was whether, as a fifth phase,
the policy henceforth identified with Mr. Heath would be
persisted in.

M. de Gaulle's veto closed the first chapter of the European
Movement and threw open the various possibilities of a new
one. Some of us had worked, for example, on the international executive committee of the major voluntary body
working for a unified Europe, the *Nouvelles Equipes Inter-
nationales,* of which Georges Bidault, Bidet, Robert Schuman, Adenauer, de Gasperi and their colleagues were members or supporters. We shared the ideals of Robert Schuman
and of Alcide de Gasperi. Whether the shape was (as
Schuman said) to be federal, or functional, a great experiment was to be made, changing the meaning of sovereignty,
reducing the risks of war, certainly visualizing itself as part
of a wider Atlantic Community, accepting the NATO
framework, and emphatically neither exclusive nor anti-
American.

One merit of the functional approach, as distinct from the
patently political, federal approach of total commitment,
was that one could see what the commitments were likely to
be in Coal and Steel, in Atomic Energy, maybe in Transport
and such technical matters, and one was not so likely to
discover novel and wide-ranging commitments, e.g. in foreign

policy which the electorate had not earlier seen as implicit when it had to confront the "States' rights" limitations in federal policy.

If this novel experiment, with which Britain could be associated, undertaken as a sample in a limited and manageable area, could succeed, with gradually increased pooling of sovereignty, then it would be an effective model for the wider "free world" area, with its trans-Atlantic, American, Australasian (or maybe Indian) constituents.

However, it appeared that this plan, despite much sprinkling of "political holy water" about universal amity, was now repudiated with arrogance in Paris; and a significantly different Gaullist plan was substituted, her relation to which Britain had now to consider. To some, such as Mr. Edward Heath, soon to be Prime Minister, this new plan, especially after the coming of Pompidou, did not seem to offer obstacles, such as the Press could seize upon, to a plan on which his own ambition was set.

Although this is not a technique which usually commends itself in major business mergers, some (not only Conservatives) urged that Britain should commit itself to EEC and to the Brussels European Commission first, and then negotiate afterwards. One calculated propaganda technique was to speak to the electorate on the hypnotic assumption that Entry had "already as good as taken place", so it was "too late to argue"—even with a popular majority against it. So much for democracy. To others the objections might not seem categorical, especially in an Atlantic political framework; but the dangers, in an issue so vital for the whole future of Britain and the Commonwealth, still required unambiguous consideration and realistic confrontation.

De Gaulle himself, it has to be added, in his last years as President, instead of saying (as he had done) that "the time will come soon when the British will themselves thank me for keeping them out", had to modify, even if reluctantly, his objections to any Anglo-Saxon adulteration of his plans for Continental Union. Britain, he reflected, might be seduced into some subsidiary liaison with the Continent, stirred by anti-American jealousy reminiscent of that of the older Vienna against Berlin. As for the General's successor, M. Georges Pompidou, he seemed to be more flexible, subtle and apparently compliant.

The policy of the small Liberal Party in Britain has been entirely consistent since the days of the Second World War. It is a strong supporter of the United Nations and of "European" Union, many of its members having been European Federal Unionists, and hence engaged in fratricidal feuds against Clarence Streit's organization in those earlier days. There is therefore here no comparison with the four or five phases of Conservative policy. On the contrary, the Liberal Party has officially supported "immediate entry" and a policy of "tarrying for none". This explains why, although in opposition, discarding Lord Randolph Churchill's maxim that "it is the duty of an opposition to oppose", it was prepared to contribute the vital ten votes which, at a critical moment, placed the Tory government of Mr. Heath in power. However Mr. Thorpe has damned the present CAP.

In the case of the British Labour Party its present position is liable to misrepresentation, owing to its earlier unwillingness officially to back any unqualified policy of political or economic union, as distinct from support for the international United Nations, or to put a Union policy into the forefront of its official programme.

A detached benevolence towards the drawing together of the nations of Continental Europe in the causes of regional peace, characteristic of the Britain of the post-war period, was expressed not least by Attlee, although for ideological reasons not equally by Dalton and Aneurin Bevan. For these there was a suspicion of anything about which Winston Churchill might be enthusiastic—just as, even at Fulton, there was suspicion about Churchill's alleged "imperialism". If one could get (and presumably electorally maintain) a "Socialist Europe" or "Third Force" in this special sense, then indeed, even for Aneurin Bevan, a European Union would be "a good thing". It was no small reservation. Attlee's basic hope lay in developing "World Law", embodied in a declaration made at Versailles.

The outlook for the most part, as also with many Conservatives (although Sir Anthony Eden is, as stated, on record as an Atlantic Unionist), was vaguely insular. Against this, however, had to be set certain counterbalancing factors.

Immediately after the war the dominant figure in British foreign policy, as Labour Foreign Secretary in close accord with Clement Attlee, was Ernest Bevin. And Bevin, far from being a "European", even to the point of support for the U.S. Department of State's myopic policy, then enthusiastic for the plan of thrusting Britain, willy-nilly, into Europe, was on the contrary not only a vigorous backer of NATO policy and of W.E.U., but also of an Anglo-American "special relationship" as the effective executive basis of NATO.

A decade and more later, some prominent members of the Labour Party—George Brown, with his euphoric enthusiasm, and Michael Stewart, inclined to take the advice of his Civil Service officials, with others such as Roy Jenkins—were outspoken, in the 'Fifties and 'Sixties, in their support of instant European Union. Their enthusiasm ran even to the point of advocating Entry first and negotiation afterwards. Here M. Pompidou and his admirer Mr. Heath were almost outdone. A profound and, it should be added, entirely admirable belief in the need for the erosion, in the cause of peace, of archaic (and often traditionally Germanic) attachment to ideas of absolute national sovereignty, inspired them. The trouble was that, concentrating on too narrow a region, they risked producing merely a new power conflict, while breaking up a wider association already in existence or in embryo, such as, first the British Commonwealth and, then, the Atlantic Community or Commonwealth.

George Brown—like, to the recorded amazement of Attlee, Herbert Morrison before him—strongly desired to be Foreign Secretary. Harold Wilson, on the record, was under heavy political pressure to become a convert to George Brown's views, although Lord Wigg states they were not his own. Both Brown and later Stewart became Foreign Secretaries; and hence for a significant time the official voice of Britain expressed the personal views of Lord George Brown. Nevertheless, subsequent events were to show that these were emphatically not the same as the recorded vote and view of the Labour Party. Lord George Brown resigned.

Further, there was the specific risk that the uncritical acceptance of EEC policy, as understood by Gaullists in Paris, would spell the endorsement of an exclusive, Paris-centred interpretation. This could in effect be uncooperative with NATO, inclined away from America as "different", destructive of the entire concept of an Atlantic Community, and marking the beginning of its collapse. Schism between the Eastern and the Western spheres, between Europe and America, would wreck the very security which the Atlantic Alliance sought to provide.

Clement Attlee, before he died, was specifically hostile to the Common Market plan. "If he stops our joining the Common Market he will have repaid what he owes us."* His successor, Hugh Gaitskell, gave only a strictly qualified and conditional support. What mattered were the terms. Here, however, it was skilful tactics for the *enragés* pro-Marketeers—politicians, businessmen, above all journalists—to cloud or muddy-up the issue, whether at the ideal or material level. The whole plan could be presented as scarcely controversial, almost fustian economic book-keeping—indeed a mere Customs Union. It was the economic terms alone which, for tactical reasons and in the best of klieg-lights, were first emphasized by Harold Macmillan.

Nevertheless, in time these factors receded in importance as the more tricky issue of the political framework came to the fore, where Britain might be thrust into the position—to Gallic joy in some quarters, the ambition of nine centuries thus fulfilled—of becoming a satellite of France. Needless to say, here the more prudent French politicians were guiltless of emphasizing the advantage. De Gaulle suspected some English trick to frustrate his own plans and take charge, or to play "Trojan horse" for the Americans.

Harold Wilson, originally "a Commonwealth man", appreciated, as Churchill had certainly done, that the position of Britain and the Commonwealth was not quite the same, historically or in actuality, as the interests and history of Italy or Germany, our recent opponents in arms. Their Continental history was profoundly different and their actual interests might be the converse. What was good for the one was not equivalently good for the others—something the *enragés* Europeans never grasped. And although, in the early days of the European Movement, men such as Bidault would readily point out that France had her own non-Continental over-seas interests in the new-born *Communauté Française,* their comparison of the Gabon Republic with Canada and Australia was, as I have said, not entirely convincing. The self-important journalists who accused Wilson of the sin of "sitting on the fence", did not hesitate to attack him no less viciously when he patently "got down from off the fence" and did so, even more sinfully, on what their inspiration and editorial interest assured them was "the wrong side". In point of fact the then Prime Minister had not "sat on

For God's Sake, p.413.

the fence" Like Gaitskell, he recognized that there were two
sides to the case: the issue was not of the desirability of
European Union but of the undesirability of risking—as
even Macmillan had said—a "widening of the Atlantic".
Temperamentally, moreover, Wilson preferred "to keep his
options open". (Disraeli had advised the same.) In the words
of a recent commentator on Lyndon Johnson, "the principal
ingredient of his procedure was . . . on any major piece of
legislation never make a commitment on what will pass"*.
Bide the right time. If George Brown could succeed, in spite
of all difficulties, good. If not, George could resign. He did.
Roy Jenkins also later quit the Shadow Cabinet.

Wilson, in brief, tolerated in 1970 the declarations of
George Brown on a policy on which the Party had as yet
reached no clear official position, major conditions attendant
on Entry still being unclear. This did not yet mean that the
exclusion of Britain from EEC was to be tolerated merely
because, in his dictatorial way, General de Gaulle "chose to
give No for an answer", *motu proprio,* a position intolerably
arbitrary and indeed insulting, although fully intelligible in
terms of French plans for a Europe of which France would
be the centre-piece.

When at last the issue, so crucial for de Gaulle, could no
longer be postponed but was thrust into the foreground, the
Conference decisions of the Labour Party were made plain
on July 17th, 1971, in Westminster Central Hall and were
reiterated in the vote at Brighton in October, 1971, and
again, in October, 1972. The Party Conferences confirmed a
view which repeated the conclusion of public opinion polls.
These showed usually around 47% "against" and fewer "for"
(Opinion Research Centre Poll, 17th October, 1971) and
made clear the majority sentiment of the country†. A national poll published on January 1st, 1973, the official date
of Entry, still showed a plurality against Entry (39%, with
23% expressing no opinion).

There was here no question, on the basis of these votes
and polls, of that "whole-hearted" enthusiasm for Entry into
Europe to which Mr. Heath, in his Election campaign—the
actual Election Manifesto had cautiously almost duplicated
the Labour one—had pledged himself, as a condition of

* Harry McPherson : *A Political Education,* Atlantic-Little Brown,
1972, p.158.

† *For God's Sake, supra* pp. 417, 448-50.

Entry and as the basis of his policy, were he to become Prime Minister. Even if, on examination, the enthusiasm was not to be seen, the fact that he was elected (not least on other issues) was held, as with President Nixon in another context, to be authority enough. After all, in his pre-Election addresses he had made a special point of the bluff honesty of his Party, and of its dedication, unlike others, to the truth†.

Labour Party reservations were made quite patent in Harold Wilson's speech (referred to above) at the Special Party Conference, in the Central Hall, Westminster, of July, 1971.* The relations of the EEC with America were one major item in what had to be assessed—and to this and to the Atlantic Alliance I shall return—although the immediate economic programme received more journalistic attention.

Nevertheless when, in January, 1973, the dramatic and art critics of Britain turned their attention to the "banging of the drum" by the bankers for "Europe"—in what the dramatist Mr. Osborne called "Fanfare for Cheltenham" and the critic Mr. Richard Cork called "Fanfare My Eye"—Mr. Cork went astray in terming the whole matter "propaganda for the enlargement of a trading club". Much more than just a mere Customs Union was in contemplation. What was at issue was the future of the British nation and the nature of its relations with the Western world. In what world was it to live?

iii

By November, 1972, Labour's sometime Minister of Defence, Denis Healey, was to assert that Entry was going to have a disastrous effect on food prices. Admittedly, the higher prices were permitted to rise before the leap of Entry, so as to make less likely an outcry on Entry.

Such a consideration as this last might be held to be cynical and to erode "credibility", but was yet consistent in tough tactics with the Heath government's initial stance, as a matter of principle and economic philosophy, of radical opposition to "Socialistic" price controls when, later, this "fundamental economic principle" was discarded and credit taken for the imposition of controls. Indeed these successful price controls were one of the major factors in producing an

† *Times Guide to the House of Commons,* 1970, p.27.

* The text of my memorandum to Mr. Wilson on this Conference will be found in *For God's Sake,* pp. 448-9.

apparent economic advance, although it was counter-balanced by an increased trade deficit of £81m. (Dec., 1972). (Control by means of a regulation by the Chancellor of the Exchequer of the value of money, based on the relation of wages and dividend rates to the graph of the G.N.P. and of production, which I have discussed and advocated elsewhere, was no official part of the contemporary scheme.) Indeed, despite the expected economic advantages of Entry, prices soared also in the Continental heaven of Europe. Although one factor of propaganda value for entry was the "economic miracle" of Germany—with Germany's peculiar advantages in a restricted Defence Budget—the economic situation of Italy as a member of the Common Market has been the reverse, and no recommendation at all.

Mr. Barber, Chancellor of the Exchequer, was able to say (2 December, 1972) that, despite all the publicized strikes, "output per man in British industry has been rising far faster than in most other major industrial countries, faster than in Germany, faster than in France, faster than in Sweden, faster than in the United States . . . Britain is now achieving one of the fastest rates of expansion in our history . . . Bang the drum for Britain." The interesting but odd point is that this miracle had been achieved *before* Entry— in the last days of Harold Macmillan economic disaster had been prophesied unless there were immediate Entry— whereas the countries of the Six had nothing comparable to show.

Nevertheless, the confidence of some British industrialists that, after Entry and in a few years, they will be sitting on top of the European economy, certainly no part of the plan of the original Six and scarcely pleasing to French or Germans, would seem rather to indicate the self-confidence which goes before a fall. Admittedly, along with M. Aaron in France, the British property men were, in France and Belgium, doing pretty well for themselves. The Hudson Institute in New York indeed produced a report (January, 1973) drastically in the opposite sense. It assuredly required courage, or what in some circles is called *chutzpah,* to "bang the drum" when British Overseas Trade, under the Tory administration in 1972, fell to its lowest point since 1957.

The chief Tory negotiator, Mr. Geoffrey Rippon, concurred with Healey in the same week that prices were going to rise still higher. They have. The Government's policy in restraint of wages and prices may be successful. But one factor in price rise has been not just wages, but the rise of import costs from Europe. (Indeed the world was so affluent that it was determined, demand outstripping supply, to eat more!) Fortunately exports to N. America have been maintained.

The Director of Research at—which is significant—the British Advertising Association, Mr. Harold Lind, wrote (11 January, 1973):—

"There is only one way in which housewives in Britain are ever likely to see relatively cheap food again and that is if a British Government was prepared unilaterally to abrogate the CAP. All they need to do is tell their partners that as good Europeans they are deeply in favour of a Great, United, Peaceful, Cuddlesome Europe, yet they cannot see why this should commit them to an agricultural system ruinous to British consumers in particular, and to the economy in general.

"Of course it will be pointed out by pro-marketeers that such an action would result in the EEC breaking up, or at least in our expulsion from it. This may well be true, although it is not quite as much a foregone conclusion as most pro-marketeers would suggest.

"But if this does happen it will prove conclusively that the EEC, far from being the bright, hopeful, new political concept its supporters hope for, is merely a rather inefficient economic system centred round an indefensible agricultural policy.

"In this case, I can see no reason why anybody in this country should wish us to be a member of the EEC . . .

"It hardly needs saying that we can expect no move to abrogate anything while Mr. Heath is Prime Minister. He had devoted himself single-mindedly to the task of making Britain a member of the EEC on any or no terms and with any or no public support."

Indeed a case might be made for advocating support for EEC on principle while, in view of French intransigence on CAP, inviting France to quit the EEC, just as with *nonchalance* France had quit NATO . . . In this primarily economic controversy no one has shown more forcibly and in detail that outstanding contemporary economic experts are opposed to EEC in detail, as much as the earlier ones were in favour on principle, than the Rt. Hon. Douglas Jay, M.P., sometime President of the Board of Trade (*S. Express*, 13 August, 1973). British Trade deficits with the Continental

The shine and glamour of the earlier vision of a glorious economic benefit for Britain, directly due precisely to Entry but at an unspecified date in the future, accompanied by possible economic *bons-bons* in the short run, were now tarnished.

It must be said frankly that, as statisticians are very well aware, drawing conclusions from statistics, if better than drawing them from ignorance, is yet a most tricky art. Broadly speaking a statistician, engaged to reach certain conclusions, can reach almost any conclusion he likes, provided he may generalise from statistics of his own choosing. What matters is who aligns the statisticians. The economic experts will differ and have emphatically differed on EEC's immediate effects. Maybe the most sober conclusion is that reached by Hugh Gaitskell, himself an economist, that the economic advantages and disadvantages about balance as a 50:50 matter.

Hence the prospectus was altered. Less was heard about EEC as a necessary surgical operation to rescue the country from a desperate economic condition in 1960. Instead of statements about the immediate economic benefits, on which it was alleged that the experts were agreed and could reject lay and ignorant dissent with a dismissal gesture of contempt, it emerged that the Government experts and their supporting journalists were likely to be confronted by other economists, no less expert. Also there would have to be heavy financial contributions to the European Commission, a non-elective body, whose Commissioners could not indeed in any way bind the countries of their origin as such, but who had taken a double, possibly self-contradictory and criminally illegal pledge of European loyalty at Luxemburg. There would, nevertheless, it was asserted, be great protectionist benefits for the new countries—although Mr. Trudeau of Canada was (December, 1972) assured by Mr. Heath that there was no need for Canadian alarm since British policy would "not be protectionist". Again the credibility of Ed-Six, our export over import failure, has risen from £68m. in 1970 to £960m. p.a. today. The constitutional problem for Mr. Jay as for M. Lind, is how to compel Mr. Heath "to go to the country" and get a popular mandate—"to get him out"—since (unlike Mr. Nixon, who had a popular mandate) impeachment is scarcely contemplated, even if on an issue more grave for the nation, there being, moreover, no Spiro Agnew in sight, not even Mr. Enoch Powell.

37

ward Heath is eroded, as was recently that of Presidents Johnson and Nixon.

Further, there would be the immense benefit of international industrial consortia in the new Market, "global companies" or at least Continental cartels, reducing national governments to relative impotence—although at the 1972 Trades Union Conference, with representatives from 23 countries present, the need could be asserted for effective international trades unions so that "the powerful, dangerous international corporations" could be controlled . . . They "are moved by no loyalty to any particular nation and are adept at evading national efforts to regulate or control them." The London *Sunday Times* (Arthur Seldon, 3 June, 1973) was indeed bold and brutal enough to argue "Whether we should let Europe destroy our Welfare State". "The British Director-General of Social Affairs in the EEC Commission in Brussels . . . will find his Eurocrat colleagues making little or no allowances for British experience with the Welfare State in their theorizing on social policy for the years ahead."

Of the future benefits, one could not indeed be more specific, precisely because they were "long-term". The trouble indeed with "long term" benefits is that one cannot say too much about them because one does not know how long the term is. But there would be, it was argued, certainly the benefit of a market of at least 250 million consumers. It would constitute, said Mr. Heath, an industrial and financial bloc without precedent and more powerful than had ever yet been seen in the world's history, such as to make all breasts swell with pride. That an even larger bloc of around 450 million human beings, in the Atlantic Community, might also be integrated was not a theme on this occasion developed or seriously diplomatically explored, despite earlier favourable comment made in the Washington Department of State in the 'Forties.

iv

However, as was realized from the beginning, for example in Treasury discussions,* although it only emerged into the open later, the vital crux of the whole design was *not so much commercial or economic as political,* which indeed the very phrase "Union of Europe" indicated. Robert Schuman

* M. Camps : *Britain and the European Community, 1955-1963,* O.U.P., New edit. 1964, p.314.

38

had seen this, as had Walter Hallstein. As, much later on, M. Georges Pompidou was to say in an interview in December, 1972, quoted in the *International Herald Tribune*:

> "The main thing was to get a better political understanding [he emphasized the world 'political'] of the objectives of the United States, the expanded Common Market of Europe, and Japan . . . Questions of money and trade tended to divide nations, and, urgent as these questions were, they were secondary to the larger political and philosophical questions that required more discussion in the future than they had had in the last few years . . . It was essential that the major monetary and trading nations began to think about these common political objectives."

There was here, from the beginning, an ambiguity about what was meant, politically and historically, by "Europe". In view of the immense historic contribution to the civilization and defence of Europe, from the days of Henry the Navigator and of Lepanto, made by the Hispanic Peninsula, was not M. Pompidou arguably right in feeling that it would be patent historical hypocrisy to leave Spain and Portugal out? How was the word "democracy" to be related to the word "Europe"? If, again "Europe" extends to the Urals and Bosphorus, then, so runs this argument, clearly the Muscovites (unlike the Americans, Australasians and other mere "colonists" from Europe) are "European", although the Siberians are not, being merely subjects of the former Russian Empire.

Absurdly enough, a certain hypnosis of the schoolboy's map has here a magical influence. Early Greek map-makers arbitrarily created Africa, Asia and Europe—the last named after an Asian lady flown to Crete on the back of Zeus, in the disguise of a bull, and raped by him there. (The Roman provinces, such as "Africa" did not quite correspond.) Incidentally I have recently noted a map (Ortelius, 1635) of Europe including "Britannia". This country—England: Scotland omitted—is described as *"Anglo-Saxon Regio sive Saxonia Transmarina"*. . . One recalls the story of Mark Twain's *Innocents Abroad* and of the balloon navigators being able to identify the Sahara, because it was brown, brown being its colour on the school-book maps. This led Lord George Brown to the double proposition that "Britain *is* and always has been part of Europe"—for that matter it had not "got off" the world—and, furthermore, "Britain *should* join Europe". The comment may be added that, as in geography, Britain will not cease to be a mere "offshore island" by "joining Europe", but is destined by Providence to remain maritime and to see what it can make of this, just as Europe remains a peninsula and just as India (but less clearly demarcated) is part of the Eurasian terrestrial mass or "heartland".

If, however, the Atlantic Design is not only a quest for human fraternity over the widest practicable areas on the way to world government, but also a present defence of the West against "adventurist" Russian expansionism, pending effective *détente* and partnership, then the question may be posed whether this political integration of a "separated" Europe—clamouring like a neurotic patient on a psycho-analyst's couch, to find its own distinctive "identity" outside the Atlantic community—does not constitute a threat, strategically and realistically, to the Atlantic plan, and is not a deterrent but a temptation to Atlantic division, to Russian exploitation, and to strategic and diplomatic aggression. Final security as offered by SAC, is by courtesy of the Americans incongruously to remain but, as it were, politically *in vacuo*, and devoid of any decisive role in the shaping of global or European policies. Were it removed, then the costs of defence for each European nation would *rise*, not fall.

A further assumption is made that British strategic, political and economic interests and Continental interests (so far as these are posited as "united") would be identical, a most dubious proposition. There was, and still is, a penumbra of doubt, where faith fades into folly, in this whole affair of a plan without a considered political framework into which it is to be fitted.

The EEC plan, in so many respects and in the tradition of Robert Schuman and of Jean Monnet admirable in itself, can be taken as a functional experimental part, limited and manageable in area, of an over-all global or at least Atlantic plan (maybe including India, once part of the century-old *Raj,* as well as the Old Commonwealth included by its own choice) for the integration of peoples, the reinterpretation of sovereignty and the executive maintenance of peace. I once had the privilege, on board ship on a transatlantic run, of discussing his proposals with M. Monnet. They were distinguished from those of the earlier, then better known Count Coudenhove-Kalergi, put forward in his *PanEuropa,* precisely because they were less Continental and exclusive. But, in another and chauvinist interpretation, Gaullist in temper, the plan could be understood as a species of Continental Isolation, comparable with and provocative of American Isolationism—something which can be strategically set over against the non-European countries almost racioculturally, as one of three or four blocs (all "Europe" being comparable merely to the new Japan in this new order), each in rivalry with the others. This would be a rivalry which those suspicious of NATO, like the Comecon, and particularly jealous of the United States, and of any "special relationship" with the U.K., would be fools not to exploit, praising "multipolarity" for others but not for themselves.

The Union of Nations would be praised to peace-loving idealists on principle. But in diplomatic practice it would be found that what would indeed cement this union of members of a traditionally hostile group would be, not a new love and affection for "good Europeans", but a common policy activated by a very real hatred of any over-powerful potential rival, East or West. Nothing unites like a common enemy, whose every success is a humiliation.

The happiest consideration here is that the chauvinist Gaullist policy (like that of *défi*) and a deliberate and damagingly expensive break-away from NATO is not only not accepted but may be effectively rejected, and that of an Atlantic Alliance and Community re-emphasized, as the widest integration for peace at this moment available.

"Let us be honest: the special relationship is a fact, isn't it?" The remark was made to me by President Truman in 1965, in Independence, Mo. Moreover, the building, since 1926-31, of the Commonwealth, not with Roman legal rigour, as under the Treaty of Rome, but as a free and liberal association, was usually regarded in Britain as a very real contribution to world integration. For this, however, the new men felt it would be better business to substitute the new Continentalism. Outside its walls indeed a sovereign nationalism could be commended even if this was, for example, a dangerous medicine for a united Canada, but it was not to be commended at home under the aegis of Brussels. Mr. Sicco Manshold, sometime Secretary General of the European Commission, was almost tactlessly clear on this. Contumacious Prime Ministers, he urged, were inclined to look to their own peoples and, having been elected by sovereign Parliaments, would yet be summarily brought to the dock

41

before the supra-national High Court in Benelux. Calais could indeed be seen as a vision across the water from Mr. Heath's own native Broadstairs; but the new perspective shrank to N.W. Europe. Toronto and Sydney were outside a blinkered vision. For the "European devotee" in Britain both the Commonwealth and the American connection, which they misunderstood, were an inconvenient bore when not forgotten—they were, as one London journalist put it, "a yawn".

In World War II the miners' leader, James Griffiths, might exhort the Welsh miners of Pennsylvania in their native Welsh; but Mr. Roy Jenkins, in his *Afternoon on the Potomac*, notes of the 1920s, that—certainly in polite society, not in the kind that travels as emigrants—"the over-whelming majority, including leading politicians on both sides of the ocean, never crossed [the Atlantic] at all". They did not visit "the colonial sticks". This snobbery was the ruin of the old empire. Philadelphia, once the largest English-speaking city outside Britain, had become as un-known as New England. So much for the past. As to the future, America was to have a changing position in the world. Which way? "Of decreasing importance." Mr. Chou En-lai and Mr. Jenkins made the same remark. The same, it so happens, is also true of Europe.

In return for the gains of the new regional Continental world, what then were to be the political debits? It was not France, W. Germany, Luxemburg and the Continental nations, who were to pay them. The British Commonwealth was to pay. It was unfortunate in some ways that the whole British Empire did not formally end on that day when, outside the Viceregal Lodge in Delhi in 1947, I stood and watched the Viceroy's last reception, the last parade, the flag lowered, the Raj ended and the *Kaiser-i-Hind* also. It was, perhaps, a pity that there was no sharp-cut legal choice, such as General de Gaulle dictated to the African members of the *Communauté Française*. "You choose. Are you with us? Or do you choose independence and its costs, the costs of *uhuru*?"

The *habitant indigène* of Guadeloupe and of Martinique, a full French citizen, can still emigrate to England—as far as the law and the immigration officials are concerned—with a freedom which, under Mr. Heath's EEC arrangements of December, 1972, citizens of the Commonwealth, as it stood under the Statute of Westminster, that is, Canadians,

42

Australians and New Zealanders (without all the voting privileges and other rights of citizens of the Irish Republic) cannot enjoy. To put it modestly, it is not tactful that a Pakistani sitting in the British Home Office (12 December, 1972) should tell a pleading New Zealand girl that, for lack of the appropriate papers, she cannot be admitted to England. For that she has to thank Edward Heath.

There is here, in terms of the so-called "new Commonwealth", no such abrupt decision as the choice which de Gaulle gave the French Community—"In or out, which?". Some hold United Kingdom passports. Some, Commonwealth citizens, do not. The victims of General Amin's xenophobia and black racialism, victims of political persecution, were yet another case. As many as 300,000 held passports entitling them to admission to the United Kingdom, although the argument was put forward amid the muddle, created particularly by Mr. Duncan Sandys, that "they would not ever actually want to use their rights". Not ever? The Empire, now dead, in law still hangs like an albatross round the neck of Britain. The Commonwealth, conceived without due planning, is threatened with abortion. Were the immigration regulations of Britain to be like those of Canada and Australia? What of the Dominions, united into the Commonwealth, which were going to provide, all over the world, a new, concrete and institutional form of political liberalism?

Not less basic was, and still is, the issue of whether the fundamental tradition of British foreign policy is to be abandoned. As the Conservative *Sunday Times,* owned by Canadian Lord Thomson of Fleet, put the matter with idiot glee: "Tomorrow, January 1st, 1973, a thousand years of British history roll away." With the Tudors and with Cabot began the policy of a maritime nation and of looking Westward; with Cardinal Wolsey, that of keeping England's hands free. Instead of Plantaganet involvement by conquest, she would seek a balance of power which would ensure that she was the satellite neither of France, which Nelson chose to term "the hereditary enemy",* nor of the Empire and Spain. It was a policy re-enunciated as late as 1907 in the Eyre-Crowe Memorandum. Britain was still to remain free by refusing involvement in Europe, while opposing any European Power which sought to subordinate to itself the rest of

* Nelson's letter, in his own handwriting, can be seen on display in the United Service Club, London.

Europe. As "an off-shore island", it might be geographically central to a wide Atlantic Community. Here it could accept its destiny. By joining Europe, it would not cease to be still "off-shore" and out of centre. How far was this radical turn-about in foreign policy to be realized, even by the Mariner from Broadstairs?

As Mr. Edward Heath has himself said, the plans of Napoleon and Hitler were not wrong in striving, like Charlemagne, to unite Europe, but wrong in the way they went about it.* Now he and M. Pompidou would adopt subtler and better methods. There would be none of "the aggressive intent", mentioned by Eyre-Crowe, since all would already have been swallowed in, Britain herself being part of the Continental policy. This would, of course, be all for peaceful purposes, except in so far as all were irretrievably involved in a Continental plan, which could easily "turn bad", made in Brussels or Paris, to repulse intrusion into (N.W.) Europe from elsewhere. If, of course, there were, regrettably, threats of *défi* or of economic imperialism from America, then—no less regrettably and with tears—there would have to be an anti-American protectionist plan. Incidentally, worst of all would be the threat, under the pretext of "an advancing peace", from any decisive American-Russian economic collaboration (to which a Russian-German form of *Ost-politik* might be added). Such a global threat to N.Western Europe could yet appear.

Mr. Heath, exponent of the new policy of European commitments and indeed maybe of a new European isolationism, was in charge at the Commonwealth Conference of 1971, at Singapore. The Conference, without being, like the U.N., ideologically international or even Asian, was multi-racial and preserved the centuries-old contact with India. The Queen's presence, as host, although habitual at these Conferences, as "Head of the Commonwealth", was not considered by the British Prime Minister to be strictly necessary or indeed fully appropriate. It was postponed to Ottawa.

At the Ottawa Commonwealth Conference, in August, 1973, Mr. Trudeau, Prime Minister of Canada, was chairman and Mr. Edward Heath left early so as not to preclude himself from taking part in the Fastnet yachting race from Cowes, for the Admiral's Cup. Unfortunately, he was later reported as becalmed, seven miles from home with the tide

* *Vide* : For *God's Sake,* p.415.

44

running against him. It was not in doubt that he regarded the European community as more important than the Commonwealth one, a remarkable multi-racial gathering of 32 nations, not more patently in internal disagreement than EEC.

A potential political misjudgment about the Commonwealth, not least about immigration rights (December, 1972) as compared with those of Irish, Sicilians and Guadeloupans, in late 1972, speedily provoked a reaction, equal and opposite. For the progressive, or even for the reactionary-minded, the inevitability of union was no longer the theme; it was now the inevitability of neo-nationalism, new flags, new anthems. The reaction of the Australian and New Zealand electorates, with a new isolationist quality, came within weeks (December, 1972). By an odd irony, due to political folly, Australia is objecting to a form of passport which, by its reference to "British subjects" (a term which should be expunged), seems to give their citizens "second class status", an affront to their nationalism at the exact moment when the British government is seeking to acquire, in wider than traditional terms, "second class status" as merely local members of a wider entity, with higher status only in terms of being new "Europeans". The next step in this development of a narrowly European policy, which can be a new "European isolationism", can, it seems, be not only the creation of Republics of Australia and New Zealand but a grave doubt as to whether these Republics, flags and anthems changed, will choose to remain in the Commonwealth. How far will the break-up go?

In New Brunswick, Canada, Sir Max Aitken, head of that Beaverbrook Group of journals which has long tried, with tactical delicacy, to walk the tight rope between support of the Heath Government and exposure of the difficulties of EEC, said that "Britain's entry into the Common Market has resulted in an unfortunate loosening of the ties between Britain and Canada", while a recent Canadian Conservative Prime Minister, Mr. John Diefenbaker, put the matter of immigration rules, felt to be insulting, more forcibly (November 22nd, 1972): "It can only mean, certainly in Canada among our people generally, a feeling that the days of the Commonwealth as we understood it [are] virtually dead." Briefly and in summary, "Singapore, 1971" was a shame-making episode in British history and, despite much inflated talk, an unnecessary one. We have still to see what changes, if any, the Queen's visit in 1973 to Ottawa and President Nixon's visit to London and Europe, will produce, as distinct from what our local Prime Minister would like produced.

The position of the Queen herself, as Continental European political integration proceeds, becomes ambiguous. Her distinctive and justifying position is not like, for example, that of King Leopold of Belgium, but is based on being herself the symbol of Commonwealth unity amid the multiplicity of changing premiers, as Queen of England, of Scotland, of Canada, of Australia and New Zealand and of elsewhere overseas. She also, at present, enjoys a social pre-eminence unlikely to be disputed and not negligible throughout North America. Under the new Heath constitutional approach the monarchy cannot help but tend to become a kind of "fifth wheel in the constitutional coach", the logic of which points to the Queen having to contemplate abdication, whatever the public sentiment. Like popular sentiment on the Common Market, such popular opinion could doubtless be disregarded in 10 Downing Street.

This is, indeed, a suggestion so unpopular that any Heathite politician would, with delicacy, dismiss the mere mention of it as not even under discussion. He would most certainly not wish these issues of loyalty and patriotism to be discussed. Atlantic Union indeed involves an integration, but one more organic, more confederate, less legalistic, more of consultation and freedom and less of centralized dictation by a non-elective Brussels Commission. At the Continental European executive meetings the Queen of England is without a place, as merely the ceremonial head of one member country. These are gatherings of executive heads. As Herr Franz Josef Strauss pointed out, in London in 1970, to applauding British European enthusiasts, the time must come when there will be just one President of Europe—with no room for other "Heads". Presumably such a President might find as his own *vis-à-vis* the Mikardo of Japan.

It would be possible, but not easy, for Britain to occupy the position of the past Portuguese empire or of Sweden. A wider EEC could include Hungarians, Roumanians and Scots. Some people have indeed what might be described as an anti-mother complex—or else their only mother is to be identified by a Zurich bank-account. It may be—with nothing left but the language and the law and this lacking a Roman dignity—that the residue of it all in Great Britain will be the popping of twenty or more salute guns on state

46

occasions, as for some maharaja, and a parade of horse-guards, to encourage tourism, most closely comparable to the Papal ceremonial band with music in the Piazza di San Pietro in Rome, led by some music-master. May be the Vatican Swiss Guard can do better. Whether this will happen will depend upon the will of the people and their capacity to distinguish false counsels. The Gaullists are skilful enough to utilize the union of Europe to draw a clear distinction between France and *les pouvoirs anglosaxons,* patently divided, to enhance the diplomatic and cultural glory of France and even to explode its own atomic bombs for practice in other people's seas. Fortunately the Russians remain unimpressed. To date an off-shore Britain, counselled by mediocre men of little faith, if of much ambition, has only succeeded on the record in diminishing itself and in selling out its heritage for those who "would a-booming go".

v

A. J. Balfour, Churchill and Baldwin, Prime Ministers, all at various times looked with some favour on the Referendum as a constitutional expedient. "Refer-and-end 'em" was Churchill's punning slogan against the Lords. Alike in Ulster and (especially) in Gibraltar a referendum was thought to be democratic, healthy and indeed the ground of the British case. What Parliament sovereignly enacts, Parliament can indeed repeal. Treaties may be on a different and multilateral basis, but even treaties can, as with SEATO, be allowed to fall into effective obsolescence or, as de Gaulle did with the Treaty of Rome, be reinterpreted in a non-federal sense not contemplated by those who drafted them. On an issue affecting, if not irretrievably deciding, the whole future of the nation or indeed whether, in the older sense, it should—the political process completed—remain a nation at all, a referendum in any democracy would seem to be a political obligation, except in the mind of a party leader whose word has lost credibility. One cannot normally suppose that "overwhelming support" can be equated with "probable disapproval".

More informally public opinion polls—as recently as in the American Election of 1972, sometimes accurate to within a decimal point—could indicate how an official referendum would go. However, when it became apparent that the promised "overwhelming support" for the Heath-Brown policy would not be forthcoming, it was then emphasized that within Great Britain itself the whole notion of resort to Referenda was outside the Constitution and unavailable, an undesirable form of populism or pure democracy. On a technicality it was for Parliament—for the Queen, Lords and the obedient majority Party in the Commons and for its Whips, the Cabinet and indeed (he having power to dismiss Ministers), for the Prime Minister to decide. After eight years of propaganda, "the People", it was alleged, were "all confused" about what they themselves wanted to be their fate. Volatile, spineless, they had to be managed.

At a time when, according to the constitutional experts, a major political disease in the West was the "turning away from politics" of the people, especially of youth, and their proclaimed "alienation", and indignation about alleged electoral powerlessness, it was dubious political morality not merely to refuse to be instructed by a particular referendum but to ignore the steady average record of the polls. As one of the most eminent of London journalists, Mr. Robert Carvel, put it: There will not be a General Election—because the Government would lose. There will not be a Referendum—because the Government would lose.

The propaganda tactic adopted was rather to introduce a new factor: fate. The electorate was told that there was nothing they could do about it. It was all fixed up by destiny. The Prime Minister knew. As surely as Canada was part of North America, the atlas made it clear that Britain was part, not necessarily of the Atlantic Community, but of *the* Community of Europe—omitting indeed Russia, Spain, Poland, Switzerland, and a few other countries. This separation of North Western Europe from other regions must lead to world peace. This being the only way, this was the cost that had to be paid for ending, if not the quarrels of Palestine or the East, or other challenges to world peace, or the conservation of energy, at least the ancient feuds of dead Hapsburgs and Bourbons. The argument had patent imperfections and even self-contradictions.

The cheers from his electorate becoming muted, Mr. Heath, as a parliamentarian, "appealed to Caesar". Not himself personally nationally elected, like an American President, he appealed "with vigour and assurance" to Parliament which had been elected and had a mandate, if not specifically for Entry (only "to negotiate") yet a mandate in general—from the majority—for a united Tory Government. This gave what in America is called "credibility". He held a majority in the Commons of about 26, which under the Constitution appeared comfortable enough—although not much different from what Neville Chamberlain could probably have commanded if, instead of resigning, he had put matters to a vote. According to R. A. Butler, Mr. Heath was "a ruthless man"; his earlier skill as Party Chief Whip was remembered.

The alternative, of giving substance to the Atlantic Alliance or Community, was a divisive plan and did not, it was thought, have to be seriously explored. The major vote on the principle of "Entry with detail to be agreed later"—the target date for establishing, in the European Monetary Co-operation Fund, the first step for a common currency, was, perhaps not felicitously, fixed for April 1, 1973—yielded Mr. Heath a majority of 112. This appeared to the country and to the world as *prima facie* fully adequate, especially when the Labour Opposition had vainly endeavoured to brace up its forces by issuing to its Parliamentary Members a "three line whip", affirming as its own the "discuss first" policy of both the Party Conference and the Parliamentary Executive.

It is essential to our present argument that it be noted that this vote favouring accession (a) did not limit endorsement on principle to purely economic or commercial issues, whether the case for them were strong or weak, but (b) could also embrace the thesis of political integration. This could also spell (a) either the inclusion of Britain within a political Atlantic framework or (b) on the contrary, insist on the "identity" of a "European Europe", a protectionist structure, Continentalist and exclusive in basic form. (c) What it certainly did was to affirm the propriety of Entry first and of much of the Negotiation afterwards, for which, it must be admitted, de Gaulle had provided a species of precedent. These were yet, for many in Britain, quite vital issues, particularly affecting policy *vis-à-vis* the Commonwealth and the United States.

Despite the apparently adequate vote, a closer analysis reveals a reality different from the appearance. Of the Tories, on October 28, 1971, 39, in a Conservative revolt, voted against Heath's lead, implying a desire for a change of leadership, if not of leader. This, however, was more than balanced when, with 20 abstentions, 69 Labour Members, in revolt, voted with the Government. They did not follow the maxim, enunciated by Disraeli and, in 1973, cited in

Tory quarters to justify their own policy changes: "Damn your principles and stick by your Party". If they had voted, as instructed, with their own Party, then—the 69 votes being recorded on the other side and hence a 138 change-over—the Heath Government would have been 27 votes *short* of a bare majority of one. As I have said elsewhere,* "27 Labour Members that night kept Edward Heath", who had threatened resignation, "in power".

In a subsequent vote, when the question of implementing decisions was still critical and when Labour Party Members conformed to the declaration of their own Parliamentary Executive, the small Liberal Party (admittedly being always, save for one Member, pro-EEC), repudiating the principle of Lord Randolph Churchill that "the duty of an Opposition is to oppose", voted *with* the Government. It could, on balance, contribute 10 pro-Government votes, 5 moving across from opposition to support. The Government won that night by 8 votes. The Government was therefore on the first occasion sustained in power by 27 of the Labour Opposition and on the later occasion not by its own Party votes, but by the Liberal Opposition. (Under American Senatorial rules of *clôture,* on so vital an issue the Bill, on the contrary, would have required a two-thirds majority or have been talked out.) Both occasions endangered the Prime Minister's credibility.

Later still (December, 1972), on an issue where the Heath Government was rigidly bound by the Rome Treaty rules on free European migration, i.e. more migration, but when the majority in the country demanded stricter control of migration from countries which were the Afro-Asian relics of a dead Empire (but when the electorate yet wished this to be without any racialist discrimination, i.e. less migration), a new Bill was put forward. As already said, this in fact could be discriminatory, (distinguishing between European rights and "Empire passport rights") against citizens of the old Commonwealth, as understood originally by the Statute of Westminster (1931). On this occasion the Heath Government was defeated by 36 votes, i.e. by more than its entire Parliamentary majority. The "overwhelming support" seemed to be running in reverse. In the summer of 1973 a poll published by the London *Times* showed an ever more emphatic deficiency of suport for the Heath policy among the public

* *For God's Sake,* p.450.

polled. Changes might indeed be made in an unacceptable Bill, when the consequences for Westminster of certain EEC rules became apparent. But a political position was being approached of contempt for Parliament itself, as well as of easy repudiation of what had been held to be pledges. No parallel of such a Governmental defeat is to be found in this century.

In 1895 the then Prime Minister, Lord Rosebery, was defeated by the Opposition in like fashion. The Prime Minister did not challenge a vote of confidence; Lord Rosebery resigned.

III

The Fork in the Road

IMMEDIATELY after World War II, in the days of U.N.R.A., of Marshall Aid and the early days of NATO, such Secretaries of State as George Marshall and John Foster Dulles were in effective control of their Department, and there was also effective accord between Secretary and President. Of recent years the accord between the Department and the White House can scarcely be described as total, and the expressed views of some members of the Department must not automatically be interpreted as the final expression of the views of the President or of his own staff. Occasionally there has been almost a Donnybrook Fair of differences.

To non-Americans it is confusing that, inheriting the individualistic Whig philosophy of two centuries ago with its rooted antagonism to the executive power, under the American Constitution there is a separation—and indeed antipathy —of powers between Executive and Congress. Within the Executive area there are differences between the White House staff and the views of major officials of the Department of State. It can indeed be argued that the eighteenth century Constitution, preoccupied with the rights of individuals, civil rights, every legal device for the protection of endangered species of animals, is unadapted to the needs of a great nation in a modern world, as distinct from an overseas agricultural nation in effect without any foreign policy of significance, and sentimentally inclined to think isolationism to be practical policy and even a pre-condition of "the great American experiment" in egalitarian democracy and individual "natural rights".

An even more misleading impression of American policy is liable to be given abroad when the official views, although carrying international weight, are those of an officer of a previous Administration, who has now quit. Thus the policy of Mr. George Ball (certainly not to be confused with wartime Senator Joseph Ball, sponsor of international federal union), who stated strongly the theme that Britain must forthwith be urged to join in with Continental Europe, and who had himself close connections with France, should not be interpreted, for example in London, as the voice of America*. It was instead much the same as the voice, not universally acceptable, of the *New York Times,* consistent critic of two Presidents (of different Parties) in succession. Indeed it was George Ball himself who remarked that "not even Moscow could be so stupid" as to suppose that he spoke on behalf of the Administration. It is more important that Dr. Henry Kissinger proposed in writing the policy of what he called an "Atlantic Commonwealth".* It is a policy of genius.

What is true is that two threads existed and continued to exist, the first of public opinion and the second of official-dom, in American policy. Further, in the post-Marshall epoch, with its concentration on aid and reconstruction, official views themselves varied in their interpretation of public opinion.

First, as to public opinion, few people are opposed to "mother love" or to "peace and prosperity". Equally it is a safe cliché that "union" (presumably not directed against somebody else: *l'union fait la force*) "spells peace". There was a species of logic in the alleged remark of the New York hostess who, having three times introduced the Swedish Ambassador as the Swiss, when the former protested, said: "I can never make out why all you small nations don't join up." The famous remark of Mr. Henry Ford, "History is the bunk", could here be a suitable addendum. It was less naive for the well-intentioned to urge that the way to peace lay in some kind of union, federal or otherwise, of the continent of Europe, although by similar logic a federal

* Attention should be called here to Mr. George Ball's address to the Amsterdam United Europe Conference, of March, 1973, interestingly entitled "Europe's Isolationism" (reprinted in *British Atlantic Committee Newsletter,* July, 1973, pp. 14-16). Mr. Ball remains obsessed with the exclusive union of N.W. Europe. "A certain amount of anti-Americanism would be healthy if it forced Europe" (including Britain) to unite. He expresses his "extreme scepticism" about the Atlantic proposals of "the year of Europe". But it is yet "unilateralism—the new American Gaullism"—which he sees as the major threat to the earlier "spacious vision" in international relations.

* H. Kissinger : *The Troubled Partnership,* 1965-6, McGraw and Anchor, p.245.

union of the continent of North America, singularly seldom urged in Ottawa, would seem equally desirable, and even more obvious.

Further, there was a suggestion, plausible to the general public if specious, that, since the wars of the century had chiefly originated in Europe, it was logical to look to the European area as the one where an effective initiative for peace should be taken. It was the theme of the late Senator Joseph McCarthy, of Wisconsin, that the simple but honest American farmer was being entangled in European quarrels by the rise of Communism and by Communist infiltration. If, however, the quarrelsome Europeans would sensibly unite, also in a union for defence, the American citizen, soldier and tax-payer, could be spared these foreign troubles. But the argument that, since the sparks of war had in immediately preceding decades most conspicuously caused fires in the tinder of the Balkans, therefore the initiative for peace should be taken by Bulgaria or Greece, was not so plausible. Danger areas indeed existed, after 1939, from Japan to Palestine and beyond, with a clamour for peace. Not least of these was, however, not Europe, but South East Asia.

Rather it was the massive force of the Great Powers, *pax Romana* or *pax Britannica,* which had through the centuries imposed and maintained peace. Europe, by contrast, and especially the Low Countries, were known as "the cockpit". Later, after 1945, South East Asia assumed a disproportionate —and, in the words of President Nixon himself, obsessive— importance, even unduly downgrading the strategic significance of Europe.

America could, when asked for more NATO contributions for defence in Europe, stress both the weight of taxation involved for the American tax-payer and the demand on American man-power in terms of drafted youth—both these lines obviously electorally popular. Outstanding generosity was, for the public, one thing. Continuing a disproportionate commitment was another. Short of a realistic and executive United Nations "to maintain peace" (the original phraseology), a "wider community", including North America, might be the vision of remarkable statesmen such as the Democrat Kennedy and the Republican Kissinger. But, for others, politicians and public, it might seem more common sense to "pass the buck" to the Europeans to look after themselves, especially as they had come to talk so much about their own autonomy, and to concentrate upon American costly entanglements in the East.

There were indeed specific American national interests (as distinct from European pledges) involved in European defence. But, in so far as these were national, it was for American people and diplomats, negotiating with Moscow instead of being instructed by Paris, to decide strictly for themselves how these could best be protected. (To M. de Gaulle's chagrin there had even been speculations on this at Yalta.)

It is not my task to comment here *in extenso* on the Vietnam war. A reference to an apparent distortion of emphasis, over the last ten years, in American policy and strategy is enough. On D Day American troops responded to the call against Hitler, although the official government of France at Vichy, earlier approved by President Coty, gave them no welcome on landing to bring freedom. In Vietnam, again, first American advisers and then troops gave support, this time on the invitation of a friendly government, which objected to the rule of Ho Chih-Minh. What John Foster Dulles and Washington perhaps failed to realise was that Ho Chih-Minh was a profoundly anti-Chinese nationalist and that, left to himself, he would probably have set up some kind of Oriental Titoist government.

The earlier French colonial government had given Hanoi warning that it must accept French conditions. Otherwise Haiphong would be bombed, civilians included, within a matter of hours. Haiphong was bombed. The Americans took no comparable course until the last months of a twelve year war. Even when, in the last years, it was patent that the United States wished to disengage from the war on terms tolerable to her allies and, despite the atrocities attendant on all wars and the monstrous loss of life for their own Vietnamese people, it was clear that Hanoi had no intention of coming to terms short of what could be represented as victory, with even a date for the cease fire which the Americans were not to be allowed to change, a date usually the privilege of the victor to determine. The alternative was asserted to be, not negotiation, but "subjugation". There was, in America, perpetual fear that, were the war fought on swift tactics, as decisive as at Sadowa and Sedan, China and Russia would intervene. In the event this civilian panic seems to have been unwarranted. In Moscow and Peking respect was accorded, as usual, to power, not to journalists.

However, on another level, the Vietnamese war was a strategic error, upsetting the balance of world policy. As no other than Chairman Mao said to Edgar Snow, "it was too far from base" and the converse of the American strategic position in Cuba. Further, it did not command, on behalf of a remote people, about whom they knew little, the adequate support of the American people. In the words of President Nixon's Second Inaugural: "The time has passed when America will make every other nation's future our responsibility . . . just as America's role is indispensable in preserving the world's peace."

Without being consistent enough to declare themselves pacifist on principle, particular American journalists, editors, and publishers, aided by television, emphasized the horrifying aspects to be found in all wars. Television in the kitchen was indeed the novel but most effective agent for pacifist refusal to fight. The British war-time measures were tough but effective. However, in America the restrictions in wartime are different from those in Britain, and the publishers did not feel the heavy hand of authority on their shoulders. Nor did the editors receive the pink slip which told them what they could only publish at their peril. Moreover—and the highest courts declined to decide—was this slaughter, formally speaking, "a war" at all?

Here not the least of the blame must fall on what I can only term the cowardice, in relation to the electorate, of Congress. Woe betide an America where the major role in government lay in the hands of a Congress, ever prepared to continue to question but incompetent to decide. If to declare war was as immoral as the *New York Times*, the *Washington Post* and Mr. Anthony Lewis thought it was, it was the duty of Congress to denounce it and to stand on its own constitutional rights. Instead it preferred, save for the dubious gesture of the Tonkin Resolution, to "pass the buck" and to allocate to the President the responsibility and, if things turned out badly, the blame. It was neither a dignified stance nor a good example for democracy.

However, the whole issue of the consistency with strong government of the Whig doctrine of the separation of powers or, again, the novel justification of a self-appointed and so-called "Fourth Estate" of "the media", to set itself up as an established critic of the Administration of any Party, cannot be discussed here. Some would hold the claim of the Press and media to be impertinent, unconstitutional and undemocratic, and their objective to be sensation, circulation and capitalist profit; others that the unbiassed recording of events by an impartial and non-monopolistic Press, dedicated to truth and "to know all" without secrecy, is essential for democracy. What is here relevant is that the Vietnam adventure, in honouring obligations to remote governments and their peoples, produced a trauma in American opinion and, consequently, in American policy.

One consequence of the military frustration, in a position which neither supporters nor opponents of the war were prepared realistically to see as the side-show in world strategy which it was, was a reaction of public opinion towards isolationism, to a cynicism by no means new about alliances and to a feeling that America should not be entrapped in any idealistic or pretentious schemes to play world policeman or to assume the responsibilities of a world role. Isolationism is indeed endemic in the philosophy of the American public, natural alike for the Mid-Western farmer and for the recent immigrant. It has, however—and this not only since Pearl Harbour—always in crisis proved to be a minority vote and not the authentic voice of America. Those whose practical political experience in America was not least in the America of 1938-44 will not forget this. The massive electoral vote in support of President Nixon in 1972 may have been given partly for bringing the Vietnam war towards its end but it was no less because he explicitly repudiated the isolationist principle, the policy of not having a foreign policy, to which Senator McGovern appeared to give spasmodic support.

Since the beginning of the century, the United States, with the growth of its power, has moved in the opposite direction, admitting comparable world responsibilities. Roosevelt was fully committed to support for the universalism of the United Nations. Schemes which went further, if not to a federal union of the whole world, at least to one of "the Free World", emanated especially from American quarters, even if in official quarters these plans seemed to be chiefly for export to others, so as to reduce, by the establishment of "a strong Europe", Washington's financial and military responsibilities, rather than for adoption even in North America itself by Senatorial and electoral vote.

Where the fundamental division took place was between those Continentalists who saw social and political union in one exclusive Continent (not including North America or indeed Eastern Europe but, in the view of M. Pompidou, perhaps including Spain), as the goal of their effort, and those who saw the goal in at least an Atlantic confederation, called by Mr. Kissinger "a Commonwealth", something more stable than a mere alliance (an organization rightly censured as inadequate by Mr. George Ball himself)—in an "organic union"—pragmatic, involving the collaboration of the member states down even to a departmental level. This would not only maintain NATO in some form such as, for the present, a military and strategic guarantee, even while seeking "to reduce the danger of confrontation between the Great Powers", but would also enlarge the conception to that of a more than sectional and economically protectionist bloc. The effect, therefore, would be to convert the civilian second clause of the NATO charter so that, "despite profound differences between systems of government", ideologically no Soviet military forces would be such as to prevent human fraternity and friendly relations. Hence in time NATO itself could be enriched and become the substance, wide and open, of a new community or "commonwealth". The next practicable stage of this, the widest now politically practicable, is the "Atlantic Community" or, at least for some Atlanticists, the Atlantic Free Trade Area.

In so far as this latter policy, despite early advocacy and pronounced White House approval, has failed as yet to get politically under way, the cause must be found, not in the indifference or opposition of the United States Senate as such, which only in October, 1972, passed *nem. con.* in committee, a resolution framed in its favour, but in the apathy of too many individual Senators and of the House of Representatives, interested in constituency affairs to the exclusion of foreign affairs and "turned off" by disillusioning experiences in Vietnam. As a direct consequence the national interest and security of America suffer.

Even the enthusiasm for international federalism, of the days of Senator Joseph Ball of Minnesota, has faded. Americans, seeing a present trend with implications disastrous for America, do not realise that Senatorial apathy to date in the Atlanticist cause, which is left under-financed and under-organised, is precisely the reason given in Britain and in Europe for indifference to this policy. "If the Americans wish to be isolationist, let them be and we will tie in, as dear friends, with the Germans and French and Luxembourgeois."

Presidential policy, however, is clear enough. That of Woodrow Wilson and Franklin Roosevelt ranged in internationalism even more globally than the immediate practical plans of Atlanticists. Those of John F. Kennedy were stated on his European tour and more than once. In Bonn (June 24, 1963) the President—and his arrangement of words is interesting—said, "I think Western Europe and the United States, Canada, Great Britain and the Commonwealth have a major role in saving" a central core in the effort to maintain traditional freedoms.

At the Paulus-Kirche in Frankfurt (June 25) John F. Kennedy declared: "We must also look—and even more closely—to our trans-Atlantic ties. The *Atlantic Community* [italics mine] will not soon become a single over-reaching super-state. But practical steps towards a common purpose are well within our grasp." The very real danger of "the steps" tactic, apparently in good faith and innocent, is that the momentum will abate, one step will be thought enough or the second may be in reverse, and great statesmanship will be discarded in favour of jealous petty politics, on the Heath-Pompidou levels.

In a personal conversation with myself, in October, 1967, President Eisenhower said to me: "What I have always wanted is a political union, no hold barred, of the United States, the United Kingdom, Canada, Australasia, EFTA— and perhaps the Germans."* He added: "Keep the idea alive". I have to admit that he added the words (I am compelled to say that they would not be mine): "Keep out the Latins". The implication was: Do not let the Mediterranean be the centre of the new set-up.

In Kansas City (July, 1971) President Nixon expressed the judgment: "Vietnam has almost totally obscured our vision of the world". On September 29, 1971, in attacking the minoritarian Mansfield-Fulbright policy, he added: "a strong United States will continue to play a responsible role in the world". In order to advocate, not that the United States because of their hegemony should play world policeman (the danger in the United States has always been the reverse, in the trend to avoid new political responsibilities) but that others of the associated nations should contribute their share, President Nixon pledged himself to visit Europe

* *Vide*: *For God's Sake*, pp. 451-2.

59

in 1973. The purpose of this tour was to be to enunciate a strong affirmative policy, as against isolationism—not just some American blessing for EEC, but an American involvement in Atlantic policy concurrently with *détente* further East.

American Presidential policy does not lack adequate clarity, made even more clear as shown by Henry Kissinger's conduct in implementing the Nixon policy. How far this *détente* policy is welcome to France, whether on the one hand by making the role of France in *détente* less important or, alternatively, by urging France to rejoin NATO if she aspires to play a major role in joint strategy, is another matter.

The pre-eminence of the American role is strategically unavoidable, even for those for whom it is unwelcome. However, even here, the incautious expression of authoritative views may press heavily on sensitive Gallic toes. Is (it may be asked) the plan to be that European politics are to be merely "regional"—and "regional" is a European word—and the role of its member states sub-regional, whereas the policy of the United States will be "global"? Without any interest in a closer union with the United States, a "global" policy, regarded as primarily an American affair, is nevertheless intolerable. Is there to be a Nixon Soviet policy, and then a Nixon Chinese policy, and then at command and at will, hustled along, "A Year of Europe"?

Even if the Atlantic Community can offer a population and market of 400 million and EEC, the rival scheme, only 250 million, with no conspicuous economic agreement, nevertheless it can be urged by Gaullists that it is insufferable that the peace of the world should be negotiated primarily between the three Super-Powers, whether or not interest has been tepid in developing the political organisation of any group of which the European Secondary Powers would be organic members. The relegation to relatively negligible global importance of the Mediterranean Powers is unacceptable and not negotiable. Indeed, a reversion to a policy of 1900, indeed a new Charter, a revival of the Franco-Russian *Entente Cordiale* of that date, has to be considered, these two countries diplomatically dominating at least Europe between them.

ii

The policy of Germany, from the days of Adenauer to those of Brandt, has shown both adaptability and consistency.

In the early days Adenauer was concerned to bring Germany back into the main line of the Concert of Europe, by establishing close relations with France (in this his success was limited) and with Italy, and also to establish an adequate defence against Soviet expansionism.

The origins of the European Movement, as distinct from the Atlantic Movement, were found, not in Washington, Westminster or Ottawa, but in the German need to re-establish itself in the Concert of Europe by close association —with some nostalgia for the Empire of Charlemagne—with France. It was a policy to which de Gaulle gave spasmodic support, without forgetting that traditional French association with Russia. As Chancellor Adenauer said, in his Memoirs, of de Gaulle: he was capable of carrying out a good European and Atlantic policy, but just as capable of wrecking everything. Germany, as late as 1963, was still capable of attaching to the Anglo-Franco-German Treaty, in its preamble, definitions of German-Atlantic ties which de Gaulle declared to be "outrageous". According to Schlesinger, de Gaulle proposed to make West Germany choose between France and the United States. Germany remained Atlanticist. However, for George Ball, once U.S. Under-Secretary of State, to stabilize future Franco-German relations meant that Britain had also to be included.

Chancellor Brandt has adopted other means of safeguarding East-West relations from Russian hostility. But he has never fallen into the error of supposing that Paris will supply him with a better defence than Washington. Indeed the French military record since 1916 is not good. Speaking in Bonn (22nd November, 1972) at the North Atlantic Assembly, the Chancellor said: "I expect a constructive further development and not a weakening of the relationship with our American friends." His political interests, as the *Herald Tribune* comments, can be shaped to dovetail exactly with those of Washington in Paris and London. In his *Peace Policy for Europe* Brandt wrote: "Anything that might loosen the attachments of the United States to Europe or European interest is bad." The Germans, as the London *Sunday Times* (24 June, 1973) commented, are no longer prepared "to toe the line" or to accept that it is for Paris to lay down the master plan. They are rather prepared to speed up towards political unity in an acceptable fashion.

Germany is not unaware that, even with Germany omitted from any atomic agreement between the French and the

British, this joint power, of France and Britain, is still "light years behind" the resources of the Super Powers. It is a prestige toy. As to an *entente* between the Super Powers, *Figaro* comments that even "Europe" has "ridiculously little weight in the world compared with the Big Two", to which comment *Les Echo* adds the warning that "neither of the Big Two has any reason to hold dear" the European Community, which here may—but also may not—include Germany with France. (Britain is, thanks to the European association, apparently among those who choose "not to be held dear".) *Figaro* (25 April), however, adds reassuringly: French "recognised political influence perhaps does not correspond to its economic and military power, but its unique brand of diplomacy—preached for the past fifteen years—makes it a partner even with the Super Powers". The diplomacy was indeed unique in its handling of those too blind to see.

There is indeed the possibility that a Central European political bloc may develop, *excluding* atomic Powers such as France and Britain in its arrangements for European security, but bringing into association Warsaw Pact countries and breaking through the Pact's exclusions. However, it is improbable that an organisation which will be accused of Finlandization, at once so weak and so diverse, could be welcomed as making a major contribution to world peace.

iii

French policy today, and indeed since 1963, is a very different matter from German policy. The fundamental problem here is Gaullism and how far the Gaullist philosophy in foreign affairs still does or does not obtain. It is not one of France as such: it might not be dominant under a government led by M. LeCanuet or, for that matter, with a reconstruction by M. Maurice Schumann. The difficulties with a government under M. Mitterand and his coalition would be of another order.

A policy shaped by French agriculture can indeed be expected to be a constant. Even for those "inside Europe" (which some had thought to be a better negotiating position) CAP, it is flatly stated, is "not negotiable". The question is whether, having quit NATO by choice, France itself is "negotiable". The core of the problem lies in an outlook on foreign policy which is traditional and even archaic. For this very reason it is not difficult to see what are its basic convictions—convictions stated, in a fashion uncompromisingly downright, by Charles de Gaulle.

This policy has not traditionally involved any federal political union of Europe; and the implications of the Rome Treaty are boldly re-interpreted accordingly. National independence and freedom are something which the new United Europe is seen as designed to protect—although just how is not equally clear. To re-quote what Mr. Heath said in an unhappy moment, in support of his close partner M. Pompidou: Napoleon and Hitler were not wrong in their aim of the unification of Europe (with or without Moscow) but merely stupid in the way they went about it. The policy, since Louis XIV, is to assert the pre-eminence of France, if not globally, then in Europe and, if not militarily, then culturally and, above all, diplomatically. Economic assertion and *défi*, important for Pompidou, scarcely weighed so much on the rarified heights of de Gaulle's policy.

Briefly, just as the national objective under Adenauer was to restore German prestige as a great nation by wooing France into the closest alliance and even union, so the Gaullist objective, outreaching Adenauer, was to restore the prestige of France in the world, after the bitter humiliation of the Second World War (when for his taste too many of de Gaulle's fellow fighters were Communists).

This was to be done on the basis of the traditional position of France in Continental Europe, holding the Balance of Power with Imperial or Soviet Russia in a Dual *Entente*. Varied by an occasional support of Poland, this is the pattern of French policy from the eighteenth century to the twentieth. In the eyes of de Gaulle the unforgivable plot at Yalta lay in what he believed to be Roosevelt's American plan to substitute, for the older Franco-Russian *entente*, an American-Russian *détente* of the Super Powers. If there was, as in the later days of Rome, to be a double Empire, the other partner with the New Rome, which was Moscow, would be the unhappily named town on the Seine, Lutetia, Paris, France. (Admittedly, in the days of the great Roman world empire York was never quite on an off-shore island, whereas Paris was quite negligible.) If, on grounds stategic, military and economic, the cause of world peace demanded this Super Power *détente*, the cause of France could demand, to replace the "cold war", a defensive alliance of all European second-level nationalities, as against a non-European arrangement for European security, so damaging to France and to French prestige.

Here Charles de Gaulle, with his strong sense of history, most rightly felt that Britain was not to be trusted. It had too good a historic tradition of being tied in with the policy of the Super Powers to be interested in some minor European plan. Essentially Britain was *not* part of Europe. Although himself condemned to death by the official France of Vichy, blessed by President Coty, de Gaulle felt fervently that France was fighting for its life, its grandeur, for all that France had been as a nation. He had logic and he had passion.

If Europe, precisely as a continent, was being eclipsed for the first time since Marathon by Asia—and now also by America—a diminished Europe must join up in self-protection. Against that eclipse by other Continents, Europe (with Africa as its convenient and subsidized back-yard) must itself assert a Continental strength. France did indeed offer aid in Africa but, when it actually came to aid in the sub-Saharan region to French ex-colonial territories, such aid would not be given through U.N. channels but only through France's own choice, to wit the FED arm of EEC. Continentalism must be the new gospel. If, furthermore, French influence (ironically enough, restored after the war by Britain and America) was humiliated in Indochina, at least de Gaulle could later go out East to prophesy that the American intrusion must also fail as France had failed. And, if the Vietnam war did not in fact end in a Dien Bien Phu, at least France would be the host to the peace negotiators and, even if there were in January, 1973, Paris demonstrations against the Saigon Delegation, the French police need but politely regret them. The American liberals themselves could announce that the "cold war" and the era of J. F. Dulles' alliances were over. The local massacres could begin.

Moreover, France had historical interests elsewhere: in the Mediterranean as *Mare nostrum*, with North Africa as a back garden; in *la Nouvelle France;* in Quebec and even, for that matter, in Louisiana and New Orleans, although these adventures had been as much frustrated by Chatham as those in India by Clive. The official support of the French language by extensive subsidy was a cause as admirable as the erection in New Orleans of a statue of the Maid of Domrémy (done to death, as it happened, largely by the University of Paris and by the Burgundians).*

* *Cf.* Henri Guillemin : *The True History of Joan of Arc.*

These may seem to be nostalgic sentimentalities. However, it would be most diplomatically dangerous to dismiss them as mere delusions of grandeur without any power-infrastructure. Restated, not in terms of an isolated and weakened France, but of a French-shaped interpretation of the North-West European Common Market, the policy could become most effective—especially if *les pouvoirs anglosaxons*, the United Kingdom and the United States, "the flies in the European ointment", could be effectively and decisively separated and, instead of being what even Hitler himself described as one bloc, could be aligned on different sides.

Rather, it was the alternative plan, for so long favoured in Washington, of a Britain entering Europe as a Trojan horse, of a business man's Britain impudently expecting "to lead and dominate the Common Market", the established friend of America and standing with it in a "special" relation, but still able (as it could in the bygone days of Churchill) to lead a Europe pleading for re-construction—it was all this that was and could still be the "illusion".

In the later succeeding epoch of Pompidou, one possible result, it was feared, of the American-Russian *détente* could be the capture by America of that large Russian market which EEC might expect to appropriate on its own. This was no light matter. Lines of economic hostility could here all too easily develop. For the military NATO arrangements, from which France had withdrawn, Atlanticists might attempt to substitute a civilianized Atlantic Community. But the prospect was, in 1973-75, more likely to be one of keen economic warfare. "Little European" (i.e. of N.W. Europe) policy would have its "identity", its "difference", its conscious "rivalry". It has also, as M. Pompidou has so appropriately insisted, its cultural and spiritual aspects. A "Fork in the Road" would be reached, a moment of historic choice. Here patently a Britain, uncertain of its world role, would not only be a most useful ally to those engaged in rivalry with America. It would almost be correct to say that its accession could make the whole French policy viable, especially if happily supplemented by an American post-Vietnam popular weariness and mood of withdrawal from Europe, for which the political name was "isolation". In a new and unexpected sense, 1973 could be, in President Nixon's phrase, "the Year of Europe". It might also be a year of disaster.

Even more dangerous than potential rivalry over the nearby Russian market, resulting from a Russo-American *détente,* is world rivalry in oil and energy supplies. Here, as in other conflicts, a firm understanding between the Super Powers based, if not on friendship—although the U.S.A. and the U.S.S.R. have never actually fought a war—but on interest, and on dialogue, not dictation, might arguably provide the surest way to world peace. It might also do the opposite.

The sad history of the secondary Powers, and especially of the petty States, from the days of the quarrels in the Balkans to those of the executive ineffectiveness of the United Nations Assembly, is based on an archaic doctrine of absolute national sovereignty—sovereignty in impotence, and equality among unequals. A new technique may be needed for dealing with the claims of monopolistic economic wealth put forward by those (not least the oil-producing countries) who rely on a static international law of territorial or marine rights. This new technique would be a safeguard against the trivial use of political power, but implies an international consortium which only the Super Powers can maintain. Reaction against the Super Powers can be reaction against strategic internationalism. This has been one element in the conflict between Dutch and French aims. But any country which still champions neo-nationalism can expect support and allies among the smaller countries and therefore can have the capacity to make trouble. The internationally minded Dutch are an honourable exception. Nevertheless the idea of multiplying Super Powers in number, until they become only marginally superior and powerless to take decisions, is not the way to peace. As the *Herald Tribune* wisely said editorially (30th January, 1973) on arms reduction conferences: "A rule of thumb in post-war diplomacy has been that the more nations are involved in a negotiation, the less meaningful the results."

In one diplomatic interchange on arms reduction M. Brezhnev referred to the obligations of Russian-American "partnership". The word "partnership", even more ambiguous than "alliance", may have many meanings. Unless defined, it should be avoided, even in the chorus of euphoric political rhetoric. It can mean the repudiation of the idea of the Atlantic Commonwealth in favour of breaking up NATO, and of an Anglo-French nuclear force with its own "identity", or of other forms of nationalist multi-polarity. We could have a Europe, not united in itself, but at least "identified" and standing en bloc against all Continental outsiders, including the United States, however much "a friend and partner".

However, the course of history may not follow quite this route. France may play in the West the Great Power part projected for Japan in the East. But here "Europe" may be but subsidiary, and a façade for the diplomatic pre-eminence of France. The Hudson Institute is a somewhat sensational body, well-advertised and working on contract, which recently projected that Britain required a new Great Depression or even a revolution to arouse it to life and modernity. Likewise it has (January, 1973) plotted out a future for France when France, thanks to superior non-egalitarian, non-comprehensive education, relying on largely technical excellence, will achieve a G.N.P. twice that of a Britain which, by 1985, will lag in the ninth place among the economic competitors of the world and behind Spain and Austria. France will be the world's third richest nation. By this time and amid such strenuous competition the very European Community itself will probably—according to the Hudson Institute—have broken up, leaving Britain and Germany as economic allies against French dominance.

I am not myself an expert in Futurology and I must leave this exercise in it for others to analyse, while noting that it has very strongly commended itself to the felicitously named M. Messmer, Premier of France. Some comments are yet permissible. If France, operating through the EEC, is to emerge—surpassing the earlier "German miracle" of the days of Dr. Ehrhard—as a kind of Superstar among States, it is odd that it was so economically disturbed by the international difficulties, in 1973, of the money-market and by the difficulties of monetary union. The EEC was no less disturbed, American devaluation being termed, by the EEC Commissioner for Financial Affairs, "a grave American challenge" and a threat—even called by the official spokesman, "insupportable"—to Europe. This resentment, however, was balanced by the Danes who held that they had not been equitably consulted by the Commission and by the Finance Ministers of the major EEC countries.

There is, however, yet one other possibility for the future, maybe supported by still more solid evidence. It is no mere speculation that, under a democratic system, the time surely comes for Party changes. Few prognostications in politics are more certain. The most recent French elections indicate that, after so long a period in power for the Gaullists, another

Party conformation will in due time take over. In terms of the entire Atlantic Commonwealth—to use the Kissinger phrase—especially if characterized by a Soviet and Chinese *détente*, it might not matter much. The Germans would doubtless even more openly look to Washington. The situation, however, would be different were all economy and policy built around a N.W. Europe organization in which France held a central and indispensable place.

In an interview in the London *Times* (12th February, 1973) M. Pierre Messmer advanced the view, in some ways politically alarming but also revealing, that the world of politics divides itself into "men of government" (including men like himself, a former Colonial Governor), with insight into the "advanced industrial society" of the future—possibly competent in what *Le Monde* called "the dictatorship of money"—and "politicians" who have "the legitimate ambition" of rising to become "men of government". The President of France cannot be expected to give way on that policy for the destiny of France to which he is pledged and mandated, thanks to any elected body of mere politicians, mere Congressmen, popular representatives. The obligation of the electorate is to accept the true faith. The option is Gaullism or catastrophe. The philosophy here is not entirely dissimilar to that of Mr. Heath, on polls and votes, and entry into the technically advantageous Common Market.

The coalition which, in terms of political realism, might be expected to replace the Gaullist group, if not sooner then later, can yet be expected to be a Popular Front, to a novel degree Communist dominated. Maybe Moscow, an unreliable parent to its own children, as the German Communists found, would in consultation with Washington restrain any excessive measure of Communist assertion. But this is an unstable basis for planning the security of Europe.

There is some cause for hilarity in contemplating the plight of American liberal gospellers of woe, who found Hanoi induced to negotiate by being pinched into acquiescence by Moscow and Peking. But this is nothing compared to the hilarity aroused were one to find Mr. Edward Heath, cool to proposals, whether Atlantic or Commonwealth, determinedly hastening, Britain in his arms, into "Europe" and then finding one of his earliest (if doubtless mind-broadening) duties was to introduce the bride to the Communist Governments of France and Italy. Final vows might be better deferred.

Personally I attach less importance than most to ideological word-battles. It is a fundamental proposition of political science that the balance swings cyclically from an emphasis on authority to a new emphasis on liberality; from stress on freedom, if excessive, to stress on authority. Nevertheless, the situation would indeed have fascinating aspects for the spectator.

IV

The Erosion of Ideology

"THE FORK in the Road" is the name given by professional commentators on strategic studies to the future international situation, not only in military but also in economic, trade and monetary matters. It is indeed a political matter. It is the time when a choice has to be made. The date when that decision has to be taken and a choice reached between an Atlantic course and a "European-Europe" course, is placed by those same experts as 1975.

It is politic to argue that no fork in the road need ever be reached. Properly regarded we see two roads at the fork coming together. Certainly there is—and this must be said with emphasis—no reason why the man who has travelled on the one, more regional, road should not be wise enough to go on to travel on the other, the main road. This same problem is sometimes referred to as the policy of "the two steps", when it is assumed that those who wish now to take the "first step" to European Union will also wish, with equal enthusiasm, once this is taken and "the fork" reached, to take "the second step" along the main road to Atlantic Union. It is, it may be held, not only impolite but also undiplomatic and "trouble-making" to refer to the Atlantic policy, as has been done, as "the Atlantic menace".

This Fork is choosing between what those in accord, if not with M. de Gaulle, at least with M. Pompidou, assert to be the right way, authentically and exclusively European, i.e. the Union of what is called "European-Europe", and something earlier, larger, but less politically emphasized. This second involves choosing, if not as a first stage yet as the always present and institutionalised goal of our journey, an "Atlantic Union"—which, incidentally, for decades has been regarded as including Australasia, North America and much of what, in some periods, was called "the free world", although this phrase (if, for example, we are to include Turkey, Portugal and Greece) may be ambiguous. Of that Atlantic World, since the defeat of the Hitlerite governments, Western Europe would have been regarded as a major part.

Incidentally, it will be noted that, for historical reasons, since World War II, the "Atlantic Union" or "Community" is the older, not the more recent, concept of the two.

For those with political eyes to see it has long been apparent that, were the North-West European world to cultivate an "identity", and perhaps even a group sovereignty, separated from the rest of the Atlantic world, then a clash between the Six or Nine of the European grouping and the residue would be not only "on the cards" but in power terms probable. Uncontrolled, such power clashes, deriving from the very nature of sovereignty, are found in the whole record of political history. Moscow would have obvious grounds for rejoicing at such a schism and clash, but some European powers also would not be displeased. This Western Europe, if united, would become a Super Power, and the United States, with a smaller population, would become less important. Canada might be neutralised, or fall into the French orbit. The only weakness in policy—and this only for the immediate strategic present—would be that the Europeans would demand both to have their cake and to eat it—to have nuclear umbrella protection and to be seen to disclaim an obligation. The amount of transAtlantic mutual obligation, let alone a sense of "community", admittedly would be minimal. Europeans would emphasise their "identity" and "autonomy" in economics, diplomacy, culture and education. But they would yet, simultaneously and for the moment, have to ask America, *sotto voce* or "psst!", to ensure that balance of arms which, however humiliating, it must be admitted is necessary for the balance of power.

In its editorial comment (quoted by the *International Herald Tribune*, June 12, 1972) *La Nation* wrote: —

"Are you Europeans, and do or don't you want to make Europe according to European, and no longer Atlantic criteria? Such is the question that France is clearly asking her various European partners."

The question is not what Italy, the Netherlands, Benelux, or still less Denmark, is asking. It is what France is asking. The United States, no longer monopolists of the nuclear bomb, it is implied, is declining. Indeed it is Mr. Chou En-lai who said, with some excuse provided by native American anarchists, that America is "decadent". For that matter, in the opinion of some British journalists and of some immigrants, Britain, faced with the dissolution of the

Commonwealth, is now "a fifth-rate Power". Defeatism and Anglo-Saxon masochism are the order of the day. In the words of Mr. Ernest Wistrich, Director of the British Council of the European Movement (*Illustrated London News*, 22 August, 1972): "We must avoid the Atlantic Menace"—although in political terms it is scarcely worth being called a menace.

La Nation continues: —

"This also is what M. Pompidou tirelessly repeats on every occasion offered to him to exchange views with the leaders of neighbouring and friendly countries."

In January, 1973—debating in Brussels with the British Minister of State, Mr. Julian Amery (who as "a cultured man", unlike Lloyd George and Woodrow Wilson, naturally spoke in French) and M. Gaston Thorn, the Luxemburg Foreign Minister—the French Vice-President of the European (Strasburg) Parliament, M. Michel Habib-Deloncle, defining what he meant in answer to the question "What kind of Europe?", said that Britain "had to decide in the months to come whether to follow Europe for independence or to follow the United States", away from this European "independence". Would it be a "51st State"?—which is nonsense—or just a "Ninth State", which is nearer to our condition?

As a former Prime Minister of Britain put it to me (and I replied that, had he not said it to me, I would have said it to him): "The danger is that we become a satellite of France", of French diplomacy. Some day indeed this N.W. Europe, as a status symbol of "independence" in the obvious dependence of its States on each other, may possess a thermo-nuclear bomb (such as the MRCA) jointly, which would give to this mutual dependence an estimable "independence", and thus make Valhalla attainable. Why worry about utopian dreams of world-citizenship—still less Atlantic citizenship? The tide of world internationalism is in reverse. The 1914-54 tide is ebbing.

An Anglo-French *mariage de convenance* has to be looked at to see whether this is really where we prefer to set up house, together holding the bomb. It is dubious whether German diplomacy will share this enthusiasm. Indeed, from the Helsinki-Geneva Conference, or later that in Vienna, may emerge a Central European union, sometimes rather confusedly called a "Finlandization", including Germany, from which the minor atomic European Powers will be excluded. However, the *New York Times* (21 May, 1972) bluntly hazarded the judgment: "For the European [?Continental] there can be little doubt that, from sheer self-defence, he must regard both [Americans and Russians, however European by derivation or claim] as aliens." This will include, of course, members of the Commonwealth also as alien.

When Mr. Heath went to Washington in 1972, the Press comment was that he spoke, not so much for Britain, as for all Europe. Recently M. Pompidou, as host to M. Brezhnev, and, by rumour proposed host to Chairman Mao, spoke for Europe. Hence Mr. Heath's sensitivity to all cordial references by President Nixon to the special interests of the two countries. This was not his mandate. However, in a more authentic sense, M. Pompidou speaks at Reykjavik to Mr. Nixon—detached from local British and German squabbles about fish—on behalf of a common "European" foreign policy. And M. Michel Jobert, with even more Franco-European emphasis, has spoken to Henry Kissinger in the same way. Britain was presented as being in the common group, despite Clement Attlee's comment: "Why should we be asked to unite today with three countries, one of which was for the second time in a generation beseeching us to rescue it from the other two?" Edward Heath had seen to that.

Commenting on the visit of Queen Juliana to Paris, in June, 1972, *Het Parool* of Amsterdam, wrote: —

"In spite of all the formal display, the visit of Dutch Queen Juliana to France was in the constellation of opposing concepts of both countries on the matter of European policy. France desires a Europe of the Europeans where national entities dominate (France a little more than the other members): a Europe which clearly moves away from the United States, and so a Europe which is more European than Atlantic-minded. The Netherlands wants a really integrated Europe, with supranational institutions enjoying far-reaching and clear authority: a Europe which, basing itself on a community of interests with the United States, is integrated in the Atlantic Community. In the French approach there is a snake in the grass however, which at first sight seems a simple demand of realism and

73

sound judgment, [but] is in fact at the same time an attempt to thrust anti-Atlantic attitudes upon Europe. The Netherlands do not want that—and, what's more, England doesn't either."

Almost exactly a year later, with half a year's experience, not of academic or partizan argument but of actual experience of EEC, the London *Evening Standard* (12 July, 1973) commented as follows:—

"Britain may be approaching a Common Market crisis if some Whitehall predictions turn out to be accurate, writes a P.A. diplomatic correspondent. Senior Ministers say privately that the next six months will be critical. For Britain's representatives in Brussels it is likely to be one long dispute after another. Whatever the attempts to conceal it, the driving force according to Ministers, is specific—Britain needs changes in EEC policy. At least one stark prediction has been made if there is failure—Britain will face the prospect of having a debit balance with the community indefinitely. The logic of this observation—offered seriously from an impeccable quarter in Whitehall—seems to be that there would then be nothing in the Common Market for Britain. The field for possible change is almost all-embracing. The common agricultural policy—admitted even by staunch pro-Marketeers to be enormously expensive for Britain when its full effects are felt—is a prime candidate. But new attitudes will also be needed towards regional policy, economic and monetary union."

Despite this statement, there is no reason why EEC should not progress and develop, provided it does so within the Atlantic framework. As no other than M. Pompidou has said (21 October, 1972): Our links [with the United States] in the Atlantic Alliance (*sic*) are so close that "it would be absurd to conceive of a Europe constructed in opposition to it". The danger, however, remains of thinking of this accord as automatic and needing no effort to sustain it.

ii

It was an observation of Lord Boothby's that, if Major-General Spears had not insisted on rescuing Brigadier de Gaulle in Paris, and this at the last available moment before the collapse of French arms, Charles de Gaulle would be a totally forgotten figure except in terms of the advocacy, along with Sir Basil Liddell Hart, of the use in warfare, of tanks which the Germans employed much more. Admittedly this would have much simplified subsequent diplomacy. There would have been no de Gaulle presidency or Gaullism; no Pompidou; no Couve de Murville or Michel Jobert. Perhaps a LeCanuet or Mitterand or Mollet. A different France—without the traditional policy that can be traced back even to Richelieu. Nevertheless, it is the tradition in policy that can provide an invaluable clue for French policy and diplomacy.

Merely to state this is to invite the response that far more was at stake than a manoeuvre of diplomacy on the chess-board of Europe, leading up to Yalta (when de Gaulle was but a shadowy figure); that France, under de Gaulle, emerged as a challenge to the future civilization of Europe; that the alliance of Adenauer and de Gaulle offered (almost) a guarantee of future Central European peace; that nothing mattered more for the peace, and indeed dignity and glory, of human civilization than the future of Europe—at least Western Europe, apart from Spain and Austria and Eastern Europe—and the leadership of France in shaping that Europe. Be it said to Charles de Gaulle's credit that his dream was not a "cosy" one of universal benign friendliness and relaxation. It had his usual military downright quality. As he himself commented—comment unfortunately repeated at the time of the Nuremberg Trial—I read it in Nuremberg—"history turns on the sword".

It is encouraging to look from this—and the irony is that here, as with Mussolini, the actual massive power was lacking to back up the imperial pretensions—to the indubitable contributions of France, not only to world colonization, but to world culture, here rivalling Italy and the self-conscious cultural superiority of China.

The century and a half after the French Revolution (if not the centuries after the Protestant Reformation) were the epoch of nationalism as a patriotic ideal. In the twentieth century, whether deriving inspiration from Woodrow Wilson or from Marx, chauvinism, now infesting Africa and parts of Asia, has suffered a setback in the advanced countries of the West, although occasionally moving below the surface of Labour "union" professions, European or otherwise.

From Ulster to South Africa there have been outbreaks, on the whole retrospective in spirit, of assertions of section-ally achieved dominance. The challenge of the *colons* continues. What, however, is interesting in this cultural warfare, be it in Celtic countries, in the actual foundation of Czechoslovakia, or in areas as far apart as India and Quebec, is the intense importance attached to language. The world is full of Levites to whom language is something almost sacred. It becomes a touchstone of loyalty. In some quarters of the world the local language, tribal, can vary from village to village. However, more often (for example in the Soviet Union) it provides no overt or tolerated cause for friction. The world languages, for convenience of communication, predominate, like Latin and the *lingua franca* of Rome, although even here, as Louis XIV well knew, an important cultural symbolism remains.

Hence it is not entirely surprising, in the rivalry of nations, that quite impressive sums of money, for reasons of culture, prestige, education and trade, should be expended on the teaching and promotion of this language or that. To some extent languages spread and grow "like Topsy". To some extent they are expanded as a matter of cultural imperialism. The English-speaking peoples here have been notoriously lazy and have allowed the spread of their language to be a matter of geographical proximity and even commercial accommodation, arousing the minimum of resentment. Indeed in the apolitical English-speaking Union the earlier notion of Evelyn Wrench that, with the Common Law, the language could provide a cultural, social, sentimental and indeed very effective bond has recently given way to the propaganda that, in order not to annoy sensitive Europeans, it should do no more—an expressed view—than provide something between a pleasant club and a species of Berlitz School of Languages, where those who do *not* speak English can come and be taught English, although not necessarily assimilated. This attitude, having nothing to do with patriotism or deeper loyalties, recalls the foolish and vain-glorious Austrian jealousies of the more powerful Germans, and a resentment of their power.

The situation with French, as the primary cultural language of Europe (even if Spanish be of wider world distribution), is different. It was not for nothing that Louis XIV (whose command of Latin was clumsy) insisted on the substitution in diplomacy of French for Latin, the court language of the Hapsburgs. (Milton was Cromwell's "Latin Secretary".) It retains, in "finishing schools" for the would-be social upper-classes, a social prestige which can have very precise political results.

This position reached a very neat expression in the formation of the EEC and European Community—and "community" itself is not easily detached from the language. After an EEC conference of Ministers, M. Georges Pompidou expressed a hope. The language of these conference had been neither German, Italian nor English but French. He expressed very properly the hope—although it had not been the practice with Woodrow Wilson or Lloyd George—that this convenient practice (M. Pompidou not speaking English) would continue. He then added, in a "throw-away" passage, which was yet electrically significant in its cultural and political implications: "after all, English is the language of America. And we must be different, mustn't we?"

iii

The reply here can be made that we are concerned with something much more valuable than French or regional European chauvinism. Or even with the glories of Racine and Molière. Our concern is with European and even Mediterranean civilization and culture: with religion and the way of living of this European Western world: with its morality, which can at need in the fight against militarism support a good and just war, and, in brief, with an ideology.

This philosophy provided the moral dynamic from 1911 onwards for the fight for "freedom" and democracy first against the Kaiser, then against Hitler, then against Stalin, if not so conspicuously against the Czar. It was the philosophy of "the hot war" and then of "the cold war". Oddly enough, however, its protagonists did not come from Southern Europe or the Mediterranean, from Berlin or Bonn, Rome, or Paris. Its protagonists were to be found mostly in Washington and in the White House of Wilson and Roosevelt, in Ottawa and in the Westminster of Asquith and Churchill.

Although Marxists, not so much impressed by traditional Europe, were opposed to some kinds of totalitarianism but not to all, most of them would yet have seen the area of this philosophy of the liberal *status quo* as that of the philosophy not only of civil liberties and of individualism, but also of free trade, trade rivalry, and capitalism, before an aggressive capitalism, primarily inspired by the profit motive, was re-presented, with a more acceptable face, and baptised by Dwight Eisenhower as "co-operative competition".

Loyalty here to the cold war, which especially for many Conservatives became the touchstone of loyalty in general, loyalty in American resistance to "Communism", which inspired the policy of ardent Presbyterian Foster Dulles and his alliances and, ultimately, the Vietnam war, not so much immoral as ill-judged, was a philosophy or crusade which began to decline in the last decade. It had its power-house in America but its champions in, for example, Adenauer in Germany and (owing to memories of his ex-allies, far more ambiguously) in de Gaulle in France. It would not be inappropriate to date the decline in the realm of ideas as setting in with the meeting between Pope John XXIII in the Vatican and Krushchev's daughter and son-in-law. The meeting of Brezhnev in the White House with conservative Republican President Nixon has been the latest expression of this cataclysmic change.

This has not spelled the rise of some new idea replacing Communism, however much intellectual criticism alike of Marx's materialist version of Hegelianism and of his sociological claim to be "scientific", rather than Messianic, may have damaged the old dogmatism. It is more to the point that a new era of social realism or pragmatism has replaced the old crusading dogmatisms. The era of ideology has given way to the era of experimental test. Nor is the social experiment that succeeds this to be confused with any cheap opportunism. As Pope John remarked, men in their youth adopt a certain militant credal intolerance. With the passing of time they continue indeed to use the old formulae, to which they believe themselves to be orthodoxly loyal. But in fact one has to judge them by their actual conduct as human beings, which may have mellowed and become more charitable and accommodating.

To mount a campaign against Communism as such is hard and can easily be either ignorant or hypocritical. The early Christian Church was communist, and this in a not specifically voluntary fashion. The monastic orders, abbeys and friaries, took vows of poverty and, for the most part, held their often prosperous estates in common. That making money, adding to capital, was an activity not only acceptable to the Lord but even a sign of divine blessing was, Judaism apart, rather a late matter of Protestant and even Presbyterian ethic, a minority view in the older Catholic culture of Europe.

It may be replied that we are, in political practice, not

concerned with what Engels called "Utopian Communism", sometimes misleadingly called "primitive", but rather— which is quite a different thing—with dubious Marxist dialectical philosophy and economic dogmas, and also with Marx-Leninism as practised in different ways under Lenin and Stalin, with orthodoxies of practice still under bitter discussion today. One consequence of this harsh system is that Kant's fundamental rule of the right to free immigration and emigration is broken and, just as the British refused to permit the free and unlimited immigration of thousands of Jews into Palestine under the Mandate as administered by Lord Samuel, so the U.S.S.R. refuses, with or without punitive fees, to allow free immigration of many into Israel. Majorities, greater in some governments than in any bourgeois democracy, nevertheless seem to be prepared to back the Politbureau, "fuller democracy", and the dictatorship of the proletariat in the Soviet Union.

It can, of course, be argued that no Communist system can compete in industry with a capitalist private-profit-motivated system, although the very existence of the contemporary Soviet military threat, in this age of the *sputnik* and of astronauts, makes this a dubious thesis.

That the Soviet system does not presume any criminal innocent until found guilty, is chary about civil rights not certified as statutory "liberties", and has no obvious crime problem but an almost Victorian public morality will not be denied. It is relevant, although probably apocryphal, that one Italian industrialist, according to the Press, supported the local Communist Party and even hoped that the Party might become the government of Italy because, in an Italy afflicted with strikes and infiltrated by anarchists, in dealing with Italian trade unionists "the Communists are the only folk who will make the bastards work".

This brings us to the fundamental issue. Under primitive conditions crusades, as between "outsider" Moslem and Roman "insider" Christian, may be fundamentally a matter of religion and cult, although also one of strategy and territorial possession. The same may be true in the irrational, fanatical and football-fan-gang fights between Ulster Scottish *colons*, upholding "the Protestant Ascendancy", and Ulster and Irish Catholics. But, even here, the issue of interest, privilege and advantage is obvious.

Nevertheless, the effort to ensure that an ill-defined democracy shall prevail against a changing communism, as a matter of principle, as distinct from any test of advantage and benefit, is scarcely worth a world war. Which side is morally superior is not a matter of patriotic belief or of logical proof, but of individual choice for those who choose to stay and even to support the country of their birth. Several bodies may seek to introduce their pattern of the good social life into the utilitarian and commercial secularism of the United States. What matters is still interest, the majority choice of advantages, and the distribution of power.

Ideologies, faiths and cultural beliefs about what is the good society may express themselves in the form, naïve or calculated, of propaganda, sincere or Machiavellian. We can have in war-time, as Malcolm Muggeridge has said, "black" propaganda or straight lies, and "white" propaganda with a larger dose of hypocrisy. But, when we turn from the "value" issue—which philosophers of the modern trend tell us is more aesthetic than indeed worthy of being called logico-philosophical—to the matter of "means" and how we control them, then the fundamental issues are those of Power and of who gives orders to whom. This has been apparent since the beginning of politics as a study. And here accommodation is possible where there is a military or economic stalemate, dictated by the facts.

iv

An accommodation between American and Russian (or indeed Chinese) interests, as a matter of mutual advantage, offers most interesting possibilities.

As I have mentioned elsewhere, the symbolic depiction of Russia as a bear has a certain shrewd truth. The bear is a friendly animal which will readily eat offered buns. However, when the buns are withheld, it can abruptly turn not only cunning but surly, and smash one's head in. A like caution is desirable in diplomatic relations. A present *détente,* dictated in part by that consistent Russian respect for power which it does not equally accord to small nations, however vociferous, is no justification for individualistic nations, who become hedonistic in their affluence, to relax and sleep.

As Kissinger has said, one has to advance beyond mere coexistence to a far closer understanding and practical *entente.* The Atlantic Treaty Organisation was established as a check, partly civilian but predominantly military, on possible Russian expansive ambitions. Any European group arrangement, justified in terms of the standardization of arms, is also cemented by the same not unjustifiable concern about Russian predominance, as well as by positive political and economic achievements.

The Russian danger totally removed, to the satisfaction of the European West, then the only justification for major and atomic armaments would be as an armed safeguard against American predominance, as distinct from the present anti-Soviet motivation. Let us, however, make the more temperate assumption. It is merely that, although doubtless this is regrettable, American and N.W. European interests may diverge, and that, the more the Franco-German nucleus predominates and the more the new "region" acquires an "identity", "personality" and patriotism of its own as *the* Community, the more likely first one and then both sides are to assume a certain intransigence in confrontation.

"The Fork in the Road" will have been reached. This Western part of Europe, always anxious to emphasise its own autonomy, will (the Russians being quiescent) be able to disembarrass itself of its resented military and atomic dependence on the United States. This section, almost certainly French guided, will be observed, even by the slowest minds, to be drawing apart from Washington and N. American influences, as a collection of *patries* pursuing a possibly unified policy on their own.

Assume that certain political leaders in Western Europe make it clear that, while they will continue to accept American military aid *faute de mieux*, and assume a situation already changing in a direction which makes such aid, e.g. in a united Germany, even less important, nevertheless in economic, technological and similar fields, including those of political infra-structure, the less American aid and interference the better—the risk, behind what M. Philippe Simonnot of *Le Monde* calls "the pretence", being that there may be too much American aid, money, interference, patronage—the question arises, especially on the global scale and without surrendering to isolationism, what should American policy be? It cannot just be a "know nothing" mood and abandonment to Congressional feuds and to the immemorial and suicidal fight between the legislature and the executive.

If Western Continental Europe will feel happier, in diplomacy, in cutting loose from any Atlantic union where the United States play the leading role, there still remains Eastern Europe. Setting aside for the moment such factors as China, Japan and a Persia which has so predominant a role in the energy field, one can visualize a Russo-American agreement, as disinterested in Western Continental European affairs as this Europe is disinterested in America. Such an agreement could go far beyond "co-existence" to an organic understanding, with appropriate consultation and annual meetings in Moscow and Washington alternately—an understanding of the Super Powers, in effective disregard of the discontented secondary Powers, which agreement could in practice control the peace of the world. There would be an end of the anarchic situation where small countries seek to be both plaintiff and judge in their own cause. If, for example, a federal union of Jordan, Israel and Lebanon were the rational solution for peace in the Middle East, such a solution there would be. Or a judgment for or against Mr. Mintoff's Maltese Mediterranean policy of bringing in Algeria and "old Carthaginian" Tunisia as part of Europe.

Here, then, is a possible answer for those who reject the political programme of an Atlantic Union or Commonwealth. In this event it would be the duty of any British statesman to see that he was on the winning side. The French would then have "to see to themselves" —which indeed would not be novel.

However, alarm about some condominium of Super Power dictatorships would be misplaced. It is true that Gallic hopes would fade of any local agreement between Moscow as the Eastern Rome and Paris as the successor of the Western Rome and focus of civilisation. But the United States is a giant, tied hand and foot against imperial centralisation, as has recently been explosively demonstrated, by a Constitution almost two hundred years old and from another age. It would be difficult to say where sovereignty lies. John Locke studiously avoided the word. Although a stronger political control in America may be required by government over empire-minded industry, not only does the whole tradition of America repudiate military imperialism but its historic structure makes it incompetent to assume it. By tradition and structure, unlike an illiberal Russia, it has to take notice of a consensus.

If danger there be, it can lie in the opposite direction. When the rumbustious Khrushchev came West to announce that, in due course, he would bury all opposition, this has to be taken as the recitation of the article of a creed. To say the opposite would be, for him, like announcing atheism at a First Communion service. (At the present moment it chances that it is on the American, anti-Nixon, pro-Sakharov side that a dogmatic anti-Platonic ideology—aggressive, Whig, permissive—is being more passionately asserted, a spark in tinder. (Sakharov is the atomic bomb pioneer.) This did not mean that the Soviet Navy would soon appear off Boston, a Communist "fifth column" parade in Washington, or Russian troops "still with snow on their boots", march through Alaska. If Khrushchev could not be expected to come to some stool of repentance and conversion, his announcement was for him just a platitude such as that "truth will prevail". Ideology would display its political power as propaganda. Nor was it necessary that the West should declare its conversion to Marxism. It would be enough that it should lose interest in its own position, even were that position one neither of imperialism nor even of condominium but of colloquium, institutionalised communication and a firm liberalism. The chair in the councils of the West would be vacant. The position of Communism is one of the support of authority on principle. That is its philosophy. The philosophy of permissive Anarchism is that of suspicion of authority and of distrust of all government on principle. A co-operativism based on the natural goodness of all men, qualified by the inherent wickedness of some men, is as far as it gets in a constructive direction. (Hence at a crunch it always suffers defeat.)

When the world knows that one Power will not support its friends, not because it has not got the man-power but because the man-power has not got the will or inclination, then the Antagonist Power does indeed rule the world. Its troops do not need to march. It is enough that they are ready to serve. It holds diplomatic dominance; what it says will be accepted. We can argue about Communism and forms of social authority. But the danger to society lies more in a permissive anarchism, incapable of offering any balance to dictatorship, than in a Communist authority with which a judicious but firm *détente* can be established, with some pragmatic asurance of what best ensures lasting peace. Compared with this, and with the terrifying evils of world war; the civil rights, even righteous ones, of bomb-making or novel-writing extrovert individuals must be seen of not the same importance. And the question of the absolute rights of emigration, urged by Kant, carries with it the issue of the absolute rights of immigration.

V

Kissinger and the Atlantic Charter

COMMENTING on the protest of U.S. Senator for Winconsin, William Proxmire, against sensational but unproven charges against President Nixon by journalists and cartoonists, beside themselves with the pleasure of being on safari after big game, the *Herald Tribune* (May 11, 1973) wrote:

> "It is evident that Watergate's effusions will not be confined within the limits of formal investigatory or judical processes. They were not released that way but by the stubborn prying of newspapermen. Once the locks were picked, there were too many assorted implications, too many people with private reasons for serving the public thirst for information, too many interests involved, to prevent unorthodox sources from providing untested, but still provocative information . . . Even the most thorough investigation by the most respected persons or agencies will, in all probability, never satisfy all the questionings about the Watergate affair. They did not in the instance of the attack on Pearl Harbour."

Much of the recent fierce discussion about the Watergate affair has not indeed turned on one of surely the most incompetent burglaries on record by burglars who could not run—or burgle—a fish shop. Some White House staff emerge indeed as betimes irresponsible schoolboys on a term-end prank and at other times as members of an old-women's knitting party, with personal and trivial malice busily making up lists of folk who must not be asked to dinner. They set to work with exposed white-tape to mark where the burglars could get in, as even the house janitor was able to remark. The whole thing was at the level of *opéra bouffe.* Rather the matter has turned on the traditional quarrel about Presidential power and privilege and on the ambitions of an incompetent Congress and of an arrogant and highly irresponsible Press.

What is at fault is a complete lack of sense of proportion in holding a balance between, on the one side, a story of janitors detecting schoolboy tricks with tape, rubber gloves and burglars' tools used by inept amateurs, on a job which, when all is said and done, in other countries could be done under the full protection of the law and no more said—countries in which, in war-time, journalists playing "the tribune", so as to cause despondency, could be executive fiat be locked up for years without appeal or compensation—and, on the other side, a cold calculation of what could issue in international peace to the immense advantage of mankind. No one could allege that, for the sake of building up some supposed American imperialism, the American press and its readers were prepared to forego probing a local scandal or to give any dangerous prestige to the President of the moment, who had rather to learn to see (in the Press) his master.

The view still expressed by Dr. Arthur Schlesinger that an affair involving threat of impeachment could be regarded as not least valuable as "soap box opera" (I quote), adding to the comic humour of nations, seems insufferably frivolous, unless one regards Dante as comedy. The fight has turned upon whether "the fundamental principles of democracy", such as the rights of Congress and of the Press, have been at stake. That the principles of democracy are best protected by the Electorate and the polls and by neither Congress nor Press is ignored. In the light of the vacillating conduct of Congress during the Vietnam war, one can only say, "God save America", if Congress took main charge of foreign policy. In Britain, for "Her Majesty's Ministers", the position of the Prime Minister is decisive. (However, quite deliberately ignoring public opinion, despite frequent repetition of pledges given, is a very different matter.) It was an interesting comment by Aneurin Bevan that "the Constitution is made to fit the people and not the people made to fit the Constitution".

Further, there is an all-American tendency, following from the supposed "right of the Press to know", to chat to the Press spontaneously, for publicity or for a consideration, or to hasten off to tell news-worthy secrets to maybe Mr. Jack Anderson, columnist who holds the key to all Privy Seals. (The sacred "right of the people to know all", however—or, as Professor Archibald Cox, prosecutor, has phrased it, "there is no exception for the President from the guiding principle that the public has a right to every man's evidence"—is flagrantly ignored when it comes to the alleged "right of the Press" to maintain the confidentiality of its own sources of information.) What may begin as a "leak", even from within official quarters, becomes a flush and soon a gusher. Abroad it weakens all capacity of American diplomacy and even military operations cease to be effective.

Has not the position, not of the President alone but of the whole staff of his advisers, even in foreign affairs, been so far damaged by the current display of American dirty linen from the journalistic flag-poles of the *New York Times* and of the *Washington Post* that any far-reaching plans for peace and international integration are discredited in advance—not just for 1973, "the year of Europe", but for a decade? It is perhaps relevant to remark that at this present time in France anyone insulting the President of France is liable to a penalty of £30,000, or a year in gaol or both.

Who knows, it may be said, what quality of leadership might not emerge next, grossly put forward by Californian salesmen and advertizing men in the mood of practical jokers and of not-so-hidden persuaders, happily called "political aborigines", about whom the late Edgar Hoover displayed singular prescience—too clever to have any ethical sensitivity and too stupid to manipulate their own plans successfully? "Anything goes." According to Mr. Andrew Tully, associate of Edgar Hoover, John W. Dean, 5th, White House counsel, was described by Hoover as "that son of a bitch" and what Hoover called "the President's Kindergarten" (including Erhlichman and Haldeman, who "don't know anything except how to sell advertizing") were people, some of whom "don't know a God-damn thing about due process of law . . . they think they can get away with murder." (Unexpectedly, Mr. Hoover has emerged from the whole affair as some kind of a wise man.) G. Gordon Liddy, central to the Watergate episode, was allegedly described by Magruder as "some kind of nut"—a type of fanatic not infrequent in political life, "debasing the standards which democracy requires".

This is not the place to discuss in depth the issue of the relations between popular democracy and foreign negotiations, which once preoccupied Morel's Union of Democratic Control. A democracy may be acclaimed as having a sovereign voice at home; but it is certainly not sole sovereign in negotiating with other sovereigns who determine their own, maybe less publicised, methods of doing business, whatever the local press may think. The pattern of the French Fifth Republic, which the French would certainly insist was democratic, would, if adopted by America, mean a great increase—and assuredly no decrease—of the powers of the President, certainly not (to use the latest phrase) "paraplegic", at the expense of Congress.

The American dispute can be seen as one peculiar to the claims of Congress, under an archaic Whig Constitutional theory of separation of powers, by implication suicidal to central power, and concerns the claims of an arrogant and inflated Press which, under the slogans of "the need to watch all government with suspicion" (even a Presidential government, directly elected by the people) and "the right of the populace to know all the truth at all times", seeks to play the role of Tribune of the People—at least until such time as its readers, bored stiff by repetition, demand that the Tribune put on some new form of entertainment.

However, "Tribune" or not, collectively the Press cannot be expected to forego its enjoyment (which is also financially profitable) of a juicy scandal, "the greatest of the century". In some not totally unimportant commercial respects, Press and Media are themselves species of the entertainments industry. Despite what can be made of the First Amendment, freedom of speech is not a moral or legal absolute. In a famous case Mr. Justice Hughes maintained otherwise.

According to the executive editor of the *Washington Post*, Mr. Ben Bradlee, if Press publicity interferes with justice to individuals then "this would be part of the price that has to be paid for a free Press" (as distinct from democratic decision). On the contrary, justice should stand; and the claims of the privately owned Press to uninhibited freedom merits a closer re-inspection than it has received. The justification for a free Press is that it enables democracy, enlightened by full and impartial information, to work.

What the pressmen of "the Fourth Estate" forget was that "democracy" as electorate, despite the directives of leading gentlemen of the Press, had massively declared itself in the President's favour at the Presidential Election and, as it were, spat in their faces. And that, in repeated polls, it had declared that, although the President's actions in particular were suspect and his popularity as low as once was Harry Truman's, the electorate, unlike the most vocal sections of the Press, did not desire him either to be impeached or to move out. The Gallup Poll of August 19th, 1973, indeed showed a 7 point rise (as against August 3rd-6th) of approval of Mr. Nixon's handling of the Presidential job. The Fourth

Estate, in brief, was not the mahout of the Electoral elephant. The pretence of the Press to be the authentic voice of the people was exploded. What it had done was to explore dark places.*

Total freedom of the Printing Press is not "a natural right" of aboriginal man. There cannot be "natural rights" about recent technical inventions; and "civil rights" are only rights accorded by the law and society. I do not know which is worse: the unrestricted freedom of the press or the radio monopoly of the BBC. Pure or majoritarian democracy is not the same as the rights of the individual—of all individuals—nor is either the same as the rights of an intrusive commercial press. Freedom of speech and press is limited by what is prejudicial to the administration of justice in the courts. Trial by Revolutionary People's Courts is dubious; and trial by newspaper and "the media" it can be urged is wrong—and should be judicially prevented in justice to those tried.

The claim is put forward that, far from being guided by capital profit and the pursuit of sensation and notoriety, a self-appointed Press should be regarded as, and have the inquisitorial rights of, a Fourth Estate. It can lecture the people *ex cathedra* about what it ought to think. Messrs. Kraft, Anthony Lewis *et al.* are appointed to tell them. It is interesting to note that in Britain the actual and true "voice

* The latest polls (Harries, August 27, 1973) have shown that 62% of those polled believed that the whole question of "Watergate" ("jam" for the Press and media) "should be turned over to the courts and allow the President to concentrate on more important things"—a direct rebuff to the East Coast American Press and its private owners. (The extent to which this group is getting "cold feet" is indicated by the *Herald Tribune* publication of David Broder's quite admirable article, "Publish and Damn Everything Else", of August 29th.) The Opinion Poll Corporation gave 53% as wanting the Congressional (Senate) hearings stopped and 54% felt that they were hurting the country. That some of these journals are not "yellow" but extremely eminent almost makes the lack of restraint more sad.

Not perhaps since Lloyd George defeated Northcliffe's *Times* by direct popular appeal has there been such a rebuke. However, in Britain contempt for public opinion by a Government kept in power by Opposition dissidents remains. My advice (*For God's Sake*, pp. 448-9), tendered to the Leader of the Opposition in June, 1971, seems to be justified.

of the people" in Public Opinion Polls (Opinion Research Centre; 15th July, 1973) holds that, in the judgment of more than a third, "journalists are among the least trustworthy of all people".

The American Press has the illusion that it, and it alone, represents the public. Patently it does nothing of the kind. The situation when President Nixon visited Peking was not without its humour. When the President and his associates and staff visited the Reception Hall in the Square of Heavenly Peace the protocol-conscious and dignified Chinese comrades put down a red carpet. As the Press corps started to walk towards it, the protocol-conscious Chinese removed it as beyond their status. Not admitted to the discussions, the members of the Press were left to interview each other and to allow themselves to be photographed providing each other with news.

There is in America, for historical reasons in what was an isolated, remote and chiefly agricultural nation, not only a detached Pecksniffian moralism, upon which George Kennan comments, but a belief that the public is sovereign, while forgetting that in other nations other peoples are likewise sovereign. The reply can be that at least American policy is "more moral", which means "more Whig"; and paladins of the Press are entitled to be more Pecksniffian, without regard to the international consequences. The lesser little dogs can assiduously sniff things out, ably aided by camera spies and by cartoonists who should be brought under the laws of libel and those of "bringing into contempt". One does not have to be a dogmatic Marxist to suspect, in "a sensational scoop" the element of profit or in rhetorical denunciation the element of personal prestige.

To have started "a relentless vendetta", in the middle of the First World War against Lloyd George for his dubious financial and even more dubious sexual activities could have been, at the time, regarded as unpatriotic and almost criminally lacking in political responsibility and sense of proportion. The sale of honours under Lloyd George was indeed terminated later, but it is wise to remember that in the days of Rosebery, with W. E. Gladstone still active, such sales took place, the Prime Minister of the day making it clear that "they did not wish to hear about them". But what, it can be said, were these personal offences compared with those of the White House at a time when the shaping of the future peace of the world is in the balance?

The general effect of this traditional American bias is that issues of foreign affairs, upon which the security of the nation depends, tend to be regarded as secondary to party domestic issues or some local interest. The comment of no other than Mr. C. L. Sulzberger, of the *New York Times*, is relevant: he wonders how the present Soviet-Pakistan situation (of 1973) "will be appreciated in Watergate-sodden Washington, with an Asian profile lower than a worm's belly". It "is unpredictable". Except in terms of effective Executive power, Moscow is not interested in Watergate peccadilloes and still less in American journalists. The abrupt Congressional termination of bombing in the Communist-occupied areas in favour of nationalist-Communist Hanoi, merely irritated Peking in its dealings on Cambodia with Washington, according to Evans and Novak.

There is no need to go so far as did the editor of the London *Times* in speaking, not just of a journalist ramp, but of an East Coast Press "lynching party"—such as had been in some measure earlier directed against President Lyndon Johnson for a Vietnam policy of which the *New York Times* and *Washington Post* did not approve, but which was now directed against Richard Nixon as also President.

By admission of White House staff itself there were "horrors", "burglaries", forced entries, wire tappings. As Messrs. Rowland Evans and Robert Novak, of the *Herald Tribune* (16th July, 1973), write, "practical Democratic politicians", sore from a recent crushing defeat, "were salivating" and indeed drooling with pleasure over the ill-judged Republican attempt, by third-rate politicians of the "ward-heeler" level, to all-too-cleverly asure a Nixon victory by "double-kill". Indeed so much was and is this so that, following the *cui bono* principle put forward in the days of the Reichstag Trial —"who stands to gain?"—a cynic might have asked whether some Democratic boss might not have tempted or bribed odd corrupt Republicans into the Watergate venture, which could destroy them.

One still asks: What precisely of value, not to say of world-shaking importance, was there in the Democratic headquarters to be burgled? The answer seems to be "nothing of significant political value". Maybe the list of a few Castro supporters. Doubtless the initial reporters, Messrs. Woodward and Bernstein, could expect to receive a journalist union's medal for the "best report of the year" and to publish a money-spinning book. But do we not have here a case of hysteria spurred by greed? Is not the best judgment that of a British judge in another (extradition) case: "The least said the better." Certainly this is what the British Government has attempted in the Dublin Littlejohns' burglary case. As Lord Carrington said, for the Government, "I see no need for an inquiry."

There was indeed another forcible entry, away in Beverley Hills, California, of the consulting room of a psychoanalyst advising Daniel Ellsberg. Ellsberg had obtained the papers stolen from the Pentagon which covered current negotiations on the Vietnam war. In Britain this forcible entry could have been entirely legal on the authority of a magistrate or of the Home Secretary. There would not have been, technically and in law, any burgling and to allege this might have led to contempt of court. In one famous case, that of Dr. Sun Yat-sen, even an embassy in London was forcibly entered under writ. But, we may ask, what decisive evidence, that could vindicate or condemn the publication of official secrets (which allegedly early reached the Soviet Embassy), are we to expect from some suspect's personal psychoanalyst's files? In Britain today the inclination is not to abolish the Official Secrets Act but to tighten it. The same might be done in America, even were that to starve the Press of its raw meat.

Although the statistics are not exact, it is estimated that French officials, in their naïve way, tap about 40,000 wires a year. The joke among Paris journalists is that they would feel insulted if their wires were too unimportant to tap. In London, Scotland Yard admits to about 6,500 wire-tappings at any one given time. What, therefore, is there to be so concerned about in Washington? Whatever legal partizans may say, such tappings and recordings seem to have been practised and authorized for decades. According to President Harry Truman's military aide and close friend, Henry Vaughan, President Franklin Roosevelt "ordered wire-taps placed on the telephones of his closest aides". During the Second World War I have every belief that my own telephone was tapped (with no clear warning noises), possibly because of suspicions of my supposed pacifist associations.

If it be said that, in Washington, this tapping as in fact carried out by the Executive is against the Law, the obvious reply is not to condemn the White House but to change ill-shaped, antiquated and unreal law. America is full of absurd restrictions on the power of government. And the greatest criminals are caught by tapping. It should be added, as final foolery, that it is now also suggested (18th July, 1973), on the fantastic farmer-boy theory, that the President is no more privileged functionally than any common citizen from the sticks, and that the White House telephone should be cut off, as being used in a fashion not consistent with the law and with T. and T. company regulations . . .

As said earlier, whether what happened in Vietnam was constitutionally "a war" is, oddly, a matter of some ambiguity on which alike Congress and Supreme Court have declined to pronounce or hedged, by mere resolutions, in pronouncing. On, however, the assumption that this event, in which so many soldiers and civilians lost their lives, *was* a war, then it is interesting and relevant to recall the British legal situation during the First and Second World Wars. During the first, *Habeas Corpus*—and according to the eminent Professor A. V. Dicey the British written Constitution lies in precisely such statutes—was suspended. During the second a more subtle technique was adopted in dealing with those who, in wide-spreading terms, might cause "gloom or despondency" and hence be, in the judgment of the Home Secretary, dangers to national security. The judgment was *his* alone; *his* certificate was enough to present in court in a *Habeas Corpus* case. The accused was not tried. He was detained—detained for a period to be decided "at His Majesty's pleasure", i.e. the same Home Secretary's, and detained without appeal and without compensation.

It is reasonable to suppose that, had the Vietnam war been "a war" and similar legislation been applied, some very distinguished owners, publishers and editors of major American newspapers would have spent much of that war in jail. Assuredly they caused alarm and despondency. Admittedly these draconian regulations, unknown in American law, were administered with great restraint. But of course these two World Wars were not on the same level of popular controversy and disapproval as were the Boer War or the Vietnam War—even if it be further conceded that this latter, despite the ignoble but calculated vacillations of Congress and the discreet ambiguities of the Supreme Court, was "really a war" and not a mere unfortunate event to which the law was blind.

It is, of course, possible to say with one commentator, reported in the Press: "Thank God for the burglaries", since they revealed and maybe cleared up so much else. However, when desiring to light a fire in a grate, to produce a healthier temperature, it is not necessary to burn the house down, as Charles Lamb remarked in his famous essay on Roast Pig, or to indulge in processes of investigation that themselves violate the ancient rule against double trial. One can even have the buffooning of trial on commercial television, with Senator Ervin present and applause allowed.

That the "dirty tricks" played by loyal but power-drunk amateurs, and the pressures applied prior to the 1972 Election, are beyond all defence will scarcely be denied. There have been too many small incidents of perjury, and lies—exposed by contradictions—have been plentiful as the weeds of the field. The alleged financial performances in Britain, of Tea Pot Dome type, of the memorable Mayor of Pontefract and his yet more opulent associates, including Mr. Poulson, the sexual deviations of a Minister of Defence who lacked the elementary modesty to keep the names of his more distinguished cousins and of Mr. Niarchos out of the list of those who had extended sympathy—all this, maybe, fades in comparison. Certainly it fades in publicity since British officialdom, judiciary and Press are more judicious than the American in playing down what should not be disproportionately played up. In the Lambton case it is noteworthy that, in Lord Diplock's Report, it is precisely the Press, seeking to bolster its sensations by the camera "which cannot lie", which comes in for clear condemnation and gets "slapped down".

In fairness it must be said that some of the various "Watergate" devices are not unique or special to Washington. The art of saying to a Parliamentary Special Committee what is calculated to mislead is not unknown to a Minister of Aerospace, Mr. Michael Heseltine; and, although technically responsible for what takes place in his Department, one may be sure that Sir Alec Douglas-Home not only does not know but makes sure that he is not informed what the hospitality arrangements for diplomats from "undeveloped" countries may be, which his officials in their skills may choose to provide according to Mrs. Norma Levy's as yet unchallenged statements—especially an official by the enchanting code-name of "Whitehead"—or was it "Whitehouse"! ? These things may be held to be deplorable by the fastidious or puritan—as indeed they can be—but the like practices are not limited just to Washington.

If all that is said about "Watergate" (residential apartments which I have visited) is true, so that not one trial but —a monster in law and a clear judicious impropriety—two official investigations at the same moment are required to deal with it, then what we have is an indictment of the American democracy which, by a landslide vote, elected a President so culpable—although it may be suspected that, under present rules, it is capable of making an equally wrong judgment in the future. Also we have an indictment of the American Constitution which, short of the extremity of impeachment, can provide no way of changing the President until the full course of a rigid tenure of office has been run.

ii

As M. Jean Monnet has commented, this whole affair, of which every item of truth and falsehood has been put under Klieg lights by Press and media, has "tarnished the American image", not least abroad. Nor must it be supposed that the self-righteous journalists, with their lofty judgments above all charge of sensationalism, thereby escape, "sea-green incorruptible". They are no "islands" to themselves, but parts of a civilization which in its entirety is now under attack, even if their role would appear, across the Atlantic, to be one of hand-wringing impotence, fanatically partizan themselves and not without a contemptible *Schadenfreude* at the discomfiture of the Head of State—pious birds all too ready to foul their own nest.

What is at fault is a complete lack of sense of proportion in holding a balance. There is a masochism about all things sad and deplorable—which is the typical American vice— catered for by the flagellations of the unspeakable. In the end a world impression is given of America as a kind of magnified Peyton Place or as something best cartooned by Norman Mailer. Mr. Mailer shared in New York a dinner party of "the President's enemies". The greatest tribute to the President is that he can claim that extremely nasty bit of work, Mr. Mailer, among his listed "enemies". (President Eisenhower also kept a list of "enemies', i.e. those who would not receive White House patronage.) Into the practices of FDR and LBJ in using the F.B.I. to investigate the behaviour of "enemies", the present Senatorial Commission decided not to enquire further as "too personal" (*Herald Tribune,* 22nd August). That man is the cousin of the ape we know. But this is not the human or humanistic fact upon which to base the diplomacy that can conduce to a better world.

Parenthetically, a civilization which rewards Mr. Norman Mailer and his jackals with applause is clearly a civilization so far decadent that, were it to be typical of the country, it would be due for replacement and the country be on the verge of moral collapse. There would be no occasion for some test of a Third World War, whether in defence of the ideology of bourgeois democracy or of permissive speech or whatever. America would already, in morals, be a defeated country. The moral leadership of its experiment would have long departed. Its culture would run the gamut from Norman Mailer to Gore Vidal and back.

The gravest part of all this is that a foreign policy of quite immeasurable importance for the peace of the world—and all American leadership in this connection—is endangered by being trumpeted at home and abroad and tied in with tawdry affairs of psychoanalysts' files and of rubber-gloved White House officials caught *in flagrante* by a janitor and the local police. Those who cannot laugh at this Bowery epic can only weep.

All of this American addiction to hasten to have a chat with the Press yields its own exquisite ironies. The Chief Executive, it is alleged, connives at the burglary of the Opposition Party's headquarters and of some obscure psycho-analyst's private files because he feels unable to continue the work of government, in war-time and later, if every secret document of State is to be leaked out maybe to the *New York Times* and maybe to the Soviet Embassy. In some countries this could lead to long prison sentences for the guilty. The consequence of a mishandled purge is that a Senatorial investigation (duplicating a legal one) is set up under Senator Sam Ervin (D., N.C.). Within a few weeks the Senator discovers that his committee's own private records of examination into burglary and leaks are being leaked (*Herald Tribune*, 21st July, 1973). The Senate Committee staff "has quietly begun an investigation of its own ranks to determine who might be responsible for leaks of committee information to news media". (Surely not Jack Anderson again?) The Committee's Deputy Counsel commented: "Frankly the leaking made Senator Ervin very irritated" . . . The *New York Times* again emerges without credit. Counsel had to appoint a special investigator into what he called "brazen leaks" to the *New York Times*.

For those who do not wish to commit the sin of the son of Noah, the "idea of the Nation as a whole" is not something that should be brought into contempt, whether by busy-beaver press-men, cartoonists (who might to advantage be made subject to the laws of libel and of "bringing into contempt") or camera-men, or by great Press and television pundits and public-relations men—or by multitudinous lawyers hungry for a brief.

In the words of the Danish statesman, Oxenstjerna, "with how little wisdom are men ruled!"; and with how much folly, by politicians and press-men alike, are the greatest plans endangered. Maybe the sooner Mr. Kissinger is out of the besieged White House, and in the Department of State as Secretary, the better.

The Presidential charisma of Roosevelt, of Eisenhower and of Kennedy is not there. Two very minor reporters of the *Washington Post*, who will doubtless write a "book of the story", have seen to that. All we can say is that this tempest, these stirrings of the witch-cauldron, have made it far harder for those who wish well to Western civilization and who find it ironic that the only balm in Washington should be provided by Mr. Brezshnev. It may be that the initiative on Atlantic proposals will now have to be taken over from an embarrassed Washington by others. But, at least, it should be possible to examine the Kissinger Atlantic proposals, which do but restate what has been advocated since the late 'Thirties, unprejudiced by the passions of the Watergate scandal and on their own merits.

How fortunate was Talleyrand in that he could assist in making a peace that could effectively last for a hundred years without, like Dr. Kissinger, having to attend to the inquisitive itch of the Press-men, to the capers of contemptible party fanatics and to the politically *louches*!

It is pure hypocrisy to suggest that democracy (conditional and "constitutional" or pure and plebiscitory) does not present dangers and even plain defects in handling the foreign affairs of nations, and this ever since the catastrophe of the Peloponnesian war.

Nevertheless Dr. Kissinger probably comes as near to political genius as this generation has seen, despite critics, none of whom is competent to take his place.

Following the Watergate affair of June, 1972, it was inevitable that those of the Press who were concerned to follow through their anti-Presidential vendetta should go on to ask whether Henry Kissinger, not only a member of the National Security Council but as one of the President's three major advisers, was not also "tainted". Could he alone stand apart from the rest?

Admittedly he, like the President, expressed doubts whether he could do his job if there were to be a series of leaks, amounting to a pipe burst, of diplomatic information, in the "official secrets" category, communicated to the general public and the other side. It could be shown that some of his own staff, by his authority, had their wires tapped—it could be plausibly said to provide them with a defence against suspicion. Kissinger could properly reply that, other Presidents apart, Franklin Roosevelt had done precisely the same thing.

This however was not enough. The leading American Press has not here been concerned with American diplomacy and status abroad; it has been Washington obsessed. The Press abroad has merely been only bored by what is permissible and what is not permissible under the oddities of American law—much that is permissible to the American Press would land a man in jail in other countries. It has been deeply concerned with American foreign policy. If Kissinger also can be shown to be "tainted", then the harpies of the press will swoop, rattling their feathers with an expectant thrill.

At a time of a patent conflict of interpretation between American and French policy, the only comment which Kraft, of the *New York Times,* can vouchsafe on Henry Kissinger's "Atlantic" foreign policy is that "the balloon . . . has been pricked. And the sound of escaping air rises". Henry Kissinger had almost become a figure of fun. With customary arrogance Anthony Lewis remarks, as if he were arbiter, that Kissinger "is entitled to compassion"—whose?—"but no longer to toleration". The real issue rather is whether Lewis should be tolerated or can be afforded. My personal answer is: "from the international point of view, No". Impeach.

On 29th April, 1973, addressing an Associated Press luncheon in New York, Dr. Kissinger put forward proposals for Western stabilization, which merited the most careful and dispassionate consideration. No one expected that this informal statement to the Press would have the finality of a Council-approved papal encyclical, beyond discussion. It was put forward rather as a considered proposal which was there for discussion and with the possibility fully visualized of disagreement on points.

When George Marshall put forward at Harvard the plan, taken up by Ernest Bevin, for what came to be known as "Marshall Aid", the impoverished Europeans were more than happy (except when inhibited by Moscow) to accept this generosity. When, in his address of 23rd April, 1973, Dr. Kissinger referred to "the Year of Europe", European Continental pride bridled at what seemed to carry an implication of patronage. The phrase appeals to Press-men in search of a slogan. It even has historical resonance. But it was possibly a flaw in tact. It was not, it was suggested, for the United States to name the mile-stone on the road. As autonomous States with their own "identity", it was for the European countries to note these decisive points themselves.

It would be nearer the truth to say that 1973 was not "the Year of Europe", but "the Year of Asia"—when the passage of Europe from the monopoly of the stage before the Russian defeat at Port Arthur, at the beginning of the century, was concluded by the monopoly of the stage being assured by the Super-Powers of Russia and China with America, with Japan and Persia in the stage-wings. This epoch can well be that of the Eclipse of so-called Europe. It is this tide which morally must and actually will roll forward. The N.W. Europeans must re-adjust themselves—and here Britain is lucky. The clear question then arises: Why attach oneself to what is fading out, when one need do no such thing?

Henry Kissinger's demand for "new approaches" was also noted. But not less significant was his statement that "the era that was shaped by decisions of a generation ago is ending". Here again the usual diplomatic touchiness was displayed. Dr. Luns, of the Netherlands, as new Secretary General of NATO, was naturally disposed to look with some approval on this young adviser putting forward a policy which envisaged support of NATO. However, as he said, among the older and tradition-conscious European countries, the response was "muted". French diplomacy at that moment, gathering together the Gallophil countries of Europe around it was doing very well, rid of NATO obligations. It saw no reason, in what appeared to be a sensational and publicity-seeking trend, for there to be any wide-flung new approaches. What need to trouble the waters? The French response, as any student of diplomacy, cynic or not, might have expected, was "cold".

What then was the alternative? Was then one consequence of *détente*, which was one of the main achievements of Kissinger's own new policy, to be the modification and even fading out of NATO so that not only the Super-Powers but each country could re-direct its armed forces to less international and, as before 1914, to more purely national requirements? In one sense the Epoch of Internationalism could end. Certainly the intimate association, since war-time, of the Atlantic Community would end, and a smaller European association, hopefully maybe negotiating with one voice in relation to the others—M. Michel Jobert is indeed the first to admit that this is not the present situation—would take its place. As one Press comment put it, henceforth Commonwealth citizens, for the whole European complex, including Britain, would be "aliens". The "European Community" to which Mr. Heath and the British had made *Joyeuse Entrée*, could not in logic believe otherwise.

It is not possible to insulate foreign policy and national authority in the international field from the supporting situation. What makes the parochially inward-looking and muck-raking diatribes of Messrs. Kraft and Lewis result in consequences so inimical to all the best hopes for world peace, and hence myopic and contemptible, is that, if this present policy, both Atlantic and of *détente* breaks down, then there will be more general defeat. There will be defeat for those political elements abroad who have risked their political lives by favouring *détente*. There will be a take-over, based on cynicism, by more militant factions, whether in Russia, China or France.

The original object of NATO was not to provoke a world-war but, by massive and centralised power, to prevent it. Hence a *détente*, however disturbing to some Europeans, is not a break with earlier NATO policy but a cautious continuation of it to success. However, a collapse of the Kissinger policy, for domestic (or what the lawyers call "municipal") reasons, means the end of the prospect of *force majeure* to maintain peace against deviants and the success of the chauvinest demand for a *force de frappe,* however inadequate and pretentious. It means not merely, as M. Jobert has explained (24th July), the end of a tactic of "a ridiculous conventional armament" (which would mean drafting more Frenchmen), but one of instant nuclear reprisal.

The question then arises: "What is to go? What is to be

begun?" The change may be so important as to be "the most profound current challenge to Western statesmanship". By referring to a new Atlantic Charter Kissinger carries reference back to the original Atlantic Charter, signed by Roosevelt and Churchill in Placentia Bay (to which Stalin later added a cynical signature), with its statement of the fundamental principles of association—but also to the Atlantic Alliance and Treaty, issuing concretely in the terms of that strategic (but also civilian) North Atlantic Organization, from which France later chose to disassociate herself on the ground that, in the self-interest of America, it impinged on the local sovereignty of France and the aspirations of French neo-nationalism.

Kissinger's appeal to a new Atlantic Charter, by a restatement of principles, would seem to seek to put a limit to this new tendency, which—although naturally satisfactory to European countries who have not only benefited by it but who even see the prospect, world peace or not, of revival of improbable national glories—yet weakens bonds that had been shaped over the decades and since two World Wars.

"Our challenge is whether a unity forged by a common perception of danger can draw new purpose from shared political aspirations . . . to deal with Atlantic problems comprehensively." In Continental Europe there is indeed the concept of a group of European nations which can enter, as they progress, precisely as a Continental group, into relations with North America. The enlarged relationship is not quite the same as the United Nations; but it is certainly not the same as the Atlantic Community earlier envisaged. For Kissinger there is, it is true, an analogy: a relation not, as for the Europeans, with an overseas America, excluding Canada, which is still alien, but "for the Atlantic nations a new relationship in whose progress Japan" (which is, like China, now scarcely to be regarded as "alien") "can share".

For Europe the European plan is to emphasize its own "regional personality", but also to assert its rightful influence on any other part of the globe where it has interests. It was perhaps unfortunate that the critics could see, in Kissinger's address, an implication that the Europeans, with their "regional personality", would be left to manage their own local affairs, with assistance balanced by their contributions, but that "global" affairs were the affairs of the United States, with its "global interests and responsibilities". Was not

France, for example, as interested as ever in an African and a Mediterranean policy?

Here the much announced "European-Europe" policy was itself in large measure at fault. As late as July, 1973, in Copenhagen there was a demand, after debate on the Kissinger Address, that the "European" countries "define a European identity", "the aim being to draw the foreign policies of the EEC member states" (this would for Denmark presumably not include Greece, which yet conspicuously proclaims the one word "Europe" on its postage stamps) "closer together".

This could go far beyond spelling economic functional arrangements. It could spell one homogenized foreign policy —in the Middle East; towards the Soviet Union; and presumably in Britain, supporting France, hell-bent on atomic explosions, against New Zealand. It can only be described as a policy ill-considered, potentially unpatriotic, damaging and disastrous. Fortunately here for once France has insisted that foreign policy shall "remain in the hands of each EEC government". In the words of Sir Alec Douglas-Home, sovereignty is indeed "control over future national destiny".

One objection raised to the Kissinger statement has been that it does not welcome the discussion and treatment of particular European-American problems separately, in technical committees, but proposes that the whole field of difference should be discussed together in plenary sessions. It is true that France has not pursued this policy of technical separation with regard to Denmark, as the Danes have complained. It has not itself stressed a division between the monetary and the economic. But, ignoring the vast and sovereign difficulties in social conditions and dismissing de Gaulle's superb political contempt for *affaires de la bourse* (for ever areas of unedifying international rivalry and chicanery, displaying the least pleasing "face of capitalism"), the contemporary French government insists upon preoccupation with these two last concerns. It is not for nothing that M. Pompidou's career has been that of a banker.

Monetarily and even economically the French bargaining position has been strong, although over-much insistence on autarchy leads to the sudden hard smack of the soya-bean . . . But in military force, as over against SAC or the Soviets, and in ensuing political competence, France is humiliatingly weak. Thus the reluctance to admit the patent truth of Kissinger's argument.

Trade and economic negotiations, Dr. Kissinger says,

"must engage the top political leaders for they require above all a commitment of political will. If they are left solely to the experts the inevitable competitiveness of economic interests will dominate the debate. The influence of pressure groups and special interests will become pervasive. There will be no over-riding sense of direction."

The pedantic and defeatist may ask why all this would-be statement of the expected Presidential lead on policy should be baptized with the resurrected title of a new Atlantic Charter. Why this term instead of something more humdrum and less alarming to the timid? Is Mr. Nixon to beat the drum? After all, the Second World War was a long time ago. Why revive that spirit? (Conversely, it may be said, if we have *détente*, unless it be a purely European security consortium of France and Russia, walking warily with Germany, shall we not give away too much?)

Interestingly enough it was M. Pompidou who, a brief while ago, urged (as already quoted) that we should turn away from the confusing maze of departmental detail, in which civil servants rejoice, and give our earnest attention to general principles and directions of policy. It was after the 23rd April Address of Kissinger that Sir Alec Douglas-Home, British Foreign Secretary, praised Kissinger for recommending a new look, "a conceptual framework", indeed "a declaration of principles". The word "Atlantic" may look back on the Atlantic Treaty and its Association. But it does also look back upon that declaration, not of topographic, but of common principles (whether or not signed by Stalin), which was proclaimed by Roosevelt and Churchill in Placentia Bay, which principles are not yet dead or repudiated. One of these principles is the imperative to pursue, and even militarily to fortify, world peace. It is unlikely that lesser men will produce a better statement. If we unfortunately no longer live in a heroic age, there is no loss in occasionally recalling it.

If the confused cannot distinguish between the two Charters, there is no reason why diplomacy should hesitate in insisting on their continuity.

If, of course, there is a motivation, personal jealousy apart, in objecting to the use of the word "Atlantic" or "Atlantic Community", instead of "alliance" or even "partnership", as interfering with an exclusive loyalty to the "European Community" (*"the Community"*), or in objecting to any continuity of principles as distinct from convenient agreements and shifting alliances, then one can see why any later agreement of the '70s should *not* be called an Atlantic Charter like its predecessor. Here we have an emphasis on different identities and different policies. Indeed, it may be said, it does not matter if the word "Atlantic" is omitted if the substance remains.

It is indeed the very nature of the objections to the Kissinger proposals, which objections imply an Atlantic negative, that provides a clear reason for an unambiguous affirmative and for the repudiation of a more parochial philosophy.

Indeed "things have changed". Just as, unreconstructed, we may continue to express our doubts about the present intentions of once trumpeted friends of the Second War, the Russians, so some maybe are luke-warm in the depth of their new-found amity for our enemies of that War, the Japanese —in Britain they were friends indeed of an earlier epoch. Even in Australia and California a marvellously new hymn is being sung, not indeed to principle but to opportunity.

However, Japan would seem to come within the new political complex in the same fashion as do the non-NATO as distinct from the NATO countries. As has been done before, since 1945, many an ex-enemy country has to be brought into "partnership". Nevertheless the emotional and cultural basis—"world citizenship" apart—of this alliance or partnership is quite different from the historical common values and sense of community which can unite the nations of the original Atlantic Charter. The basis, in the new case, is a convenient mutual advantage which, as is frequent with an alliance, can be changed when the advantage changes. It would be rash to prophesy what may be the state of Sino-Japanese relations by the end of the century.

Henry Kissinger, in his Associated Press Address, stressed —and this more than once—the importance of friendly Japanese relations, as of undeniable importance. But this does not yet mean that the association of America and Japan is just about the same in quality as America's association with the NATO Powers of Europe. To hold together the Western grouping of nations is a reason for congratulation. What is now required is an effective infra-structure of co-operation.

To achieve a *détente,* unprecedented for a quarter of a century and fundamentally for half a century, with the Soviet Union is a triumph. To add on a like *détente* with Peking reaches the level of a miracle. Despite the natural professional insistence of Mr. Edwin Reischauer, sometime U.S. ambassador to Japan, on the importance of Japan, in view of the past strained relations of Japan with China and Russia and other Eastern countries, to seek simultaneously to keep a third diplomatic ball in the air, in the sense of at the same time playing off Japanese interests, not only equally but even diplomatically more than with the other two, could risk not an even greater triumph but collapse. What matters here is merely that Japan shall not feel herself treated, economically and politically, as "an outsider".

If we are sentimentally persuaded to proceed from two Super-Powers to three, including China; and to four including a would-be united North Western Europe; and to five, including Japan—then we slip into the marsh of executive impotence of the United Nations Assembly. The whole effect of a concorde for the massive maintenance of world peace is lost. If the ground for association is merely a temporary advantage in military or economic terms, then the Shah of Persia—his country being the world's fourth largest oil producer, scarcely a Third World country along with those of the Caribbean, and crucial in energy issues—could well be brought in.

It may be true that, with "consultation", the watch word for progress towards world peace, there might perhaps have been more tact in handling the Japanese where Sino-American relations were under negotiation. It is yet equally likely that more publicity here, trumpeted to the world by a busy but irresponsible Press, could have aborted the bilateral Chinese negotiations themselves. And these were obviously more important, even if "the economic miracle" of a nation such as Japan, unburdened like Germany by defence costs, is more sensational. It is simply not true that every time one adds yet another so-called Super-Power to the list, not only for consultative but also for executive purposes, the prospects of world peace improve. The contrary may be nearer the truth. The inflated structure may be weaker, each country looking not to peace but to a chauvinist interest.

What, in these present terms, basically matters for peace is the relation of what Henry Kissinger chooses to call the Atlantic Commonwealth with the Soviet Union. Deviations from this broad plan will be divisive and can be disastrous. Lenin's sneer about "committeeism" may here have more than a grain of truth.

iii

"France's efforts to dominate in the councils of the European community have lately become more than usually disturbing, both in substance and in manner. Not since the days of General de Gaulle at his most dictatorial have her partners been so outraged as on Monday, when Mr. Jobert sent the other eight foreign ministers on a wild goose chase to Copenhagen. They were discussing co-ordination of their policies with a view to President Nixon's visit in the autumn . . . If there is to be a permanent location for discussions on foreign policy, France wants it in Paris.

"Mr. Jobert went out of his way to be off-hand about America. The formation of a European identity, he said, must proceed at its own pace without reference to America . . . Any bird trying to rule the European roost in these dangerous times would not even save its own neck."

It is important to note that this striking excerpt comes from the *Daily Telegraph*, one of Mr. Heath's strongest supporters. If the policy here condemned is not to continue then Mr. Heath perhaps has to change his own policy or to leave the conduct of British foreign affairs to those who will. The reason why Kissinger has to be supported is to be found in contemplation of the alternative. Like de Gaulle, M. Marcel Jobert has been explicit. And with M. Jobert, in his present mood, there can clearly be no compromise.

As has been stressed before, the fundamental issues today in Europe, as de Gaulle fully saw, are political, not economic. What risks will the politician take? What vision of a social order does the statesman see? Monetary and economic policy turn upon the political will. Nevertheless, it is important to note that the picture has changed and disappointed even those glorious economic prospects, not of an Atlantic market but of a European Market, which were so much advertized in the 'Sixties.

No London journal has more loyally supported Mr. Heath and his EEC policy than the *Sunday Times*. But it is this newspaper (29th July, 1973) which reports:

105

"A group of the most senior civil servants, working in the British mission to the Common Market in Brussels, have written a report to their chiefs in Whitehall saying that all the evidence of seven months membership suggests that the EEC is a disaster for Britain . . . the basic attitudes of the report are rejected, and the Government proposes to brazen it out . . . In this fraught atmosphere the most pessimistic officials are beginning to wonder whether the critics were not right all along, and whether the basic concept which took Britain into Europe was all wrong."

What will Lord Harlech reply to all that? The reply can be made—and, in quarters already deeply committed in reputation, will be urged with persistence—that, Britain having entered the Common Market in January, 1973, cannot now "as a matter of honour" get out. Something can yet be done. It is to display national displeasure with those, politicians and journalists, who got her in, "sight unseen", i.e. without the drawbacks and conditions fully examined. ("Join first and bargain afterwards.")

The defence argument here chooses to ignore that, although responsible for French adhesion, in the case of France M. de Gaulle successfully and almost unchallenged got away with a re-interpretation of the implications of the signed Treaty of Rome which quite fundamentally changed, presumably for the advantage of France, the entire character and direction of "the European Community". Emphatically de Gaulle, in Sir Alec Douglas-Home's words (16th June, 1973), retained "control over future national destiny". It ceased to be understood, as in the days of Robert Schuman, as a federal union or at least a confederate union of six or more countries, developing from a functional merger, in part, of sovereignty for particular purposes such as coal marketing and transport—which union would still regard itself as both experimental and gradual and as part of a yet wider Atlantic association. It was to be a new idea in the world, more practically effective than the pious United Nations . . .

In lieu of all this, what has been presented, at least by Gaullists, is a *union des patries*, in which sovereignty is not eroded nor individual foreign policy as yet compromised, but where economic arrangements are made greatly to the advantage of French farmer-voters, who support Gaullism of some fashion, and where the diplomatic hegemony of some

States is acknowledged under threat of blackmail that these States, if offended, will quit and break up the entire system. If de Gaulle can reinterpret the Rome Treaty, so can others, equally honourably.

<h2 style="text-align:center">iv</h2>

In his important Leffingwell Lectures for the Council of Foreign Relations, delivered in 1972 and just published,* Alastair Buchan, professor at Oxford and sometime Director of the Institute of Strategic Relations, has produced a survey which justifies the political doctrine, clearly acceptable in Middle-Power countries, of "multipolarity" and of a new "multiple balance of power". It is an argument which accords better with the European enthusiasm of 1972 than with the more experienced European disillusionment of 1973. "I hope I have said enough to impart my personal conviction that a plural world of five, possibly more, centres of major international power and influence is emerging." And why stop there?

As Buchan truly observes, here quoting from William James: "the unity is not fully experienced as yet". (Nor is it yet.) In this new era, instead of "a decline in ideological and military rivalry", as expected in the early 1960s, there has been rather, according to Buchan, a manifestation of ideological quarrels within both the Western and Eastern camps. The chauvinist nationalism of de Gaulle may have held irrelevancies and archaisms, but pluralism was accepted. Indeed, looking back, "why did the United States intervene in two world wars", its pressure in favour of European union being just utilitarian, "if not to prevent the domination of Europe by a hegemonic Power"—Germany or, for that matter, with greater success, Russia?

Since before 1914 in Hague Conferences (such as that of 1907); in 1914 with the drive "to end war"; and in the League of Nations and onwards—the major political urge of the century has been, I suggest, Internationalism and optimism about ending what Lowes Dickinson called "the International Anarchy", the European epoch of the War between the States. After the disillusionment of 1946 and later with the teethless United Nations, a more cautious but not less enthusiastic support was forthcoming for versions of

* Alastair Buchan: *Power and Equilibrium in the 1970s*, Praeger and Chatto and Windus, p.44.

"regionalism", Atlantic or European—the basic issue being which were the appropriate regions and of how wide they could be, consistent with being effective and substantial and not being what Aristotle condemned as "watery". "Which areas?" is the problem in best serving the cause of stable peace.

The question is whether "multipolarity" is not merely a more polite name for a revival of Nationalism, with accompanying "spheres of influence", or even of that chauvinism which we had hoped was dying in the advanced and more liberal countries of the world, even Germany, Italy and France—at a time when this epidemic of political cholera, passing out of the West, was becoming increasingly virulent as it moved in waves across a still uninoculated and exposed Asia, Africa and South America, not to speak of more backward lands. The problem had seemed to be that of reconciling a sound social spirit of firm local patriotism—for Rousseau the source of all civic virtues but sometimes xenophobic—with an internationalism or concept of world citizenship which required education and an evolution towards wider loyalties (not excluding the smaller) and to communities less limited than those of the village green. The fierce localism of Albania, the fanatical sectarianism of the Scottish *colons* settled in Ulster and of their no less enraged opponents, the brutal hostilities of Burundi and Rwanda, the barbarians so often prevailing against the civilized, seemed spectres from a fast dying age.

That these distortions could be presented as the trend of the future, so that even Leninism appeared more liberal, was a terrifying prospect. But, just as internationalist enthusiasm has, in the 'Forties, assumed the more cautious form of a pragmatic regionalism, could not chauvinism find a new defence, as a multiplicity of Great Powers, half a dozen or more, not in a balanced scale but as in a "mobile", decentralized, their views and immediate interests diverse and jealous, so that individual nations could, for their economic and technical advantage, group in mutual defence? On this neo-national basis not only Arabs and Africans but indeed all Europeans—or some—could associate behind their respective stockades.

Admittedly one motive for pushing forward with the economic EEC formation was a *défi*, an intensive distrust, not so much of "the American State"—the Whig-liberal tradition of America is such that the word "State" must here rather be discarded in favour of "federal union", the word "State" being suspect in any national sense—as of the altogether too rogue-free, uninhibited and wide-ranging, super-national (as with ITT) American industry with its own uncurbed imperialism in pursuit of its own profits. Here, *l'union*, or *le take-over, fait la force*. And a common threat to European industry seemed to demand an inflexible defence against the Americans in these questions, not so much of citizenship as of commerce, even when actually endangering American national policy.

If indeed the whole American outlook was "utilitarian", then there were scarcely grounds for complaint about this commercial reaction. Indeed the Department of State could cheerfully encourage what was called "European Union" as a diplomatic convenience ("did they all but have a common policy it would be easier for negotiation"). A myopic tax economy and a man-power economy could look the same way. Some of the tough and Shylock mood of the 1920s returned. But what the Department of State failed to understand was that it might be encouraging a Frankenstein (especially in a Western Europe in *entente* with Russia) that could throttle it. As Kissinger said on 23rd April, 1973, "we assumed, perhaps too uncritically, that our common interests would be assured by our long history of co-operation".

Was, the alarmed European industrialist might say, a conscious American global role, an American hegemony, imperialism, dominance in politics to be encouraged? Was not rather American economic and financial strength, and proportion of the world's G.N.P., yearly declining?

What was here forgotten was that many Americans, far from being interested in imperialism, were superbly indifferent to world politics, to a world role, to any politics beyond pump and water-gate slush.

Perhaps it was the duty of the American Government to whip in the American industrial imperialism of the American entrepreneurs and advertisers, so as to make, e.g., ITT conform with the less obnoxious lines of official American policy. But it was yet a duty little applauded and for which the sensitive need was little understood. Unfortunately it was not in line with the individualist American tradition, which regarded with dislike most political responsibilities—"un-American imperialism"—abroad. The American citizen was so shell-shocked by the notion that he might be regarded as an "imperialist", especially after an ill-conceived overseas war too far from base, that America tended to have no foreign policy at all, except the complaint that it was not America that was exploiting Europe. It was Europe that exploited America. Aptitude or not, it had no appetite for leadership, even as a chairman in consultation. It lacked the Talleyrand touch and Americans—or a vast minority—had a nostalgia for isolationism. America could simultaneously be accused in politics both of being too weak and withdrawn and of being too strong and dominant, the former usually being a political and the second an economic charge. The risk of American political imperialism is negligible.

If I understand Professor Buchan aright, he sees our contemporary world as still a Nineteenth Century world of ethnic nationalism (and certainly this last has made divisive inroads into the patriotism of the United States). Today we have "a world of intense nationalism" (p.55). This fanatical tribal barbarism can be regarded as the trend of the present and future, this surge itself being confronted, as opposite number, by a political intolerance no less fanatical, ready even to commit suicide at Masada and to invite the suicide of its allies. This atomization is to be regarded not as something to be dominated even by a new imperialism, Roman-style, or by collective security, but made a respectable and common-sense doctrine known as "multi-polarity".

To this view of the International Anarchy I am basically opposed, whether it be called "freedom", "sovereignty" or by any other name. And here the policy of the Middle Powers —and it is a view into which our smaller Britain can be seduced—can be more dangerous than that of the miniscule ones. Multipolarism once accepted, the internationalist movement ends. It means war—sanctified. It is intolerably dangerous in a Thermo-nuclear Age. It is well, as Lester Pearson indicated, that these national or baronial claimants should be held *in terrorem*, as was perceived, even in less dangerous times, from Dante to Kant.

I do not concur that "the bipolar structure of the international system is dissolving before our eyes". Strategically this is not true even in tendency; and it is carrying anti-Marxism to an extremity to suppose any total divorce practicable between modern arms, too costly even for France, and economics. As Kissinger rightly says, "the political, military and economic issues in Atlantic relations are linked by reality, not by our choice or for the tactical purpose of trading one off against the other".

Professor Buchan seems to suppose, not two or maybe (very questionably) three Super-Powers and a bi-polar "advisory position" dissolving, if not into any uniting world government, at least into a bi-polar pragmatic balance and concord, but a "mobile" gadget of five or more would-be Super-Powers, Japan one, China another, not easily to be distinguished from a row of "greatish" Powers, such as Brazil, and so across to a non-united congeries of little sovereign claimants.

My thesis is that too many small and irresponsible sovereigns backed by too many unco-ordinated but rival and ambitious Great Powers is a recipe for distrust, irritation, jealousy, adventurism and war.

"Peace is divisible" . . . This was said against those who advocated (often in far too facile fashion) "collective security". Is "every war a world war?" This is a matter of degree. Nevertheless it was the theme of "collective security", against expansive tyranny, which prevailed.

So long as our ape-cousins' race of mankind is tainted with "wild lawless freedoms" and with the original sin of what Aristotle called unlimited desire, the means also of establishing peace are going to be tainted with the defects of power. And here, to the "taint of imperialism"—especially the local imperialism of Athens and Delos and that of the Raj in India, against which Tagore protested, not that of Rome ruled by Spanish and even Syrian Emperors—the only workable alternative is that of the routine and organic consultation of like-minded nations, that organic (not despotic) union, which Lippmann and I advocated in 1940.

V

However, Alastair Buchan lays his finger on one too little noted problem, where I heartily agree with him. If it be accepted that the final touchstone in politics (and *la politique c'est choisir*)—not even the production and pursuit of wealth or the reduction of population, or social checks on pollution, but the achievement of stable peace: not Poverty, Population or Pollution—is Peace, then there are some strange consequences. There will always be comparative levels of poverty and deep-set subjective feelings of injustice where those who so feel will be reluctant to accept the discipline—on which civil justice was built up through the Middle Ages—of accepted tribunals and the due process of law. This way one ends in "jungle law", not in law's rational revision—even that (as no other than Jefferson recommended) of the U.S. Constitution. And it is perhaps especially the young who are tempted to "take the short cut".

It is one of the first fundamentals of political science that human beings are reluctant, when the utility is marginal or remote, to pay the costs. Slavery was abolished by war and *force majeure*. But how then shall war be abolished? Granted equal arms, or superior skill or cunning in guerilla warfare, or better morale, it is the more barbarous and less civilized people, the men of Ghenghiz Khan, who win against the "more sophisticated", and the more hedonist and individualist.

Nevertheless, the main task in politics is to provide protection and aid for the decent citizen, the small middle man. Solutions of the problems of poverty, pollution, population, are all here practical objectives. But, as a limited, practical, obtainable one, the preservation of peace takes priority.

The most plain, simple method of ending war would seem to be to refuse to take arms. This is what we have heard from estimable people for thirty or more years—indeed from Tolstoi. Surely we require a peace-minded population and one so educated. Even the police will be impotent if too high a proportion of the population has been brought up in bloody-mindedness. Nevertheless the best popular education will not totally abolish those who see advantage in aggression. How, then, does one meet a Stalin or a Hitler?

Even Gandhi was not a total pacifist*. He deferred to a World Court judgment and would support it. Shall we, then, be pacifists for particular wars, pacifists *ad hoc* in wars of our own choosing to protest against, "unjust wars" of our say-so? To some extent "yes". The democratic majority may refuse the call to arms. But is it unjust to support our friends? (My personal view is that America should have called an end to its "pledge to its friends" with the death of Diem and negotiated a Titoized Vietnam.) We have, following a small pacifist movement from Jaurès onwards and in pre-war Britain, seen (using the same actual Peace Pledge symbols) an amazing take-over of the greatest nation's policy —under Johnson and under Nixon—by a massive negation of war and by *ad hoc* pacifism, far more effective than the pro-Boer sympathy in Britain at the beginning of this century. Some just disliked the draft. Some had quite a solid

---

* *Vide* G. Catlin : *In the Path of Mahatma Gandhi* (1948).

disapproval of a policy that had gone wrong, directed against the politicians who had advocated rash commitments in ill-planned alliances.

There are here two routes. Buchan, I think rightly, sees (much of) "youth", especially in America, taking the semi-pacifist course. As had been said earlier, "Why die for Dantzic?" Consomols, *Hitler-junge* and Italian youth saying *"Quant'è bella giovinezza"* had all taken a wrong route when it came to judgment. In the unexpected, stinging words of the immortal Lenin: "By the decrees of God Himself, youth is stupid". Emotion in the 'Thirties had said "war". Now emotion said "peace". And, when the cool study of political means was abandoned, a principle could yet be found for this. The principle was Anarchism, one's personal conscience (as Sartre taught, with no involvement with informed and objective values). The way was to take the solitary "plunge of decision". The Kropotkin "gospel" taught the natural co-operativeness of mankind. The Bakunin "means" was of the released instincts, angry, uncivilized, uncurbed, without restraints, its violence private and sadistic.

As to the mood of disillusionment and "alienation', among the more vocal of some American youth, during the period of the Vietnam draft and of individual moral disapproval of Democratic Presidential policy, somewhat timidly Congress-supported, the most prudent comment perhaps is that these moods and fashions of what is so loosely called "youth", which are liable to change and even to moods of revulsion from decade to decade, without clear leadership but yet strong views, Press publicized by Deutschke in one direction can be outdated and followed by views no less emphatic in the other, equally complaining of impotence in getting the Government's ear. The famous Oxford University Union Resolution, between the wars, "I will not fight for King-and-country", it should be noted, did not mean that they would not fight *other* wars, for example against Hitler. The risk still remains: after Anarchism, Fascism. The sane conclusion would be that, were Anarchism our only choice, Communism would be morally better. At least it is not made decadent with hedonism and private greed and graft. It is not permissive, libertine more than liberal, lax and mastur-batory. This is not the choice yet. And with a firm and self-confident liberalism, which revises tradition with technical sensitivity, it need not arise.

The problem is whether America has the will to review

itself, discarding alike anarchism and a factitious but sacred legalism. The take-over of the world, including America, preached by Lenin and parroted as pure dogma by Khrushchev, will not come by military conquest, the planes flying from Europe, the Russian divisions marching, "snow on their boots", through Alaska. Arms may be there, but the way will be prepared by "influence". Nor need we expect a mass conversion to Marxism. "Bourgeoisification" is a more likely materialism.

The danger in the pacifist route can come from a total disillusionment; a turning away, from State politics and from party vendettas; a desire to "escape" from what has come to seem a "false reality", into music and mass pleasure (all life becoming "private"); a comfortable desire for hedonism, "not to be troubled"; above all a resolution (such as obtained among the Roman civilians confronting the Vandals) to "damn patriotism" and not "to go to the wars". It is not Communism but Anarchism that is the threat.

vi

There is another route. Logical enough as it may seem from an arm-chair, we are not yet in a position in this century to affirm world-government. Natural law, indeed, and a derivative world-law may provide a norm. Clement Attlee and others signed a declaration in its favour at Versailles. But, in the words of the famous question of Andrew Jackson to John Marshall: Who is going to execute it? Either, it seems, we shall have, again to use Aristotle's phrase, a "watery" association of which the United Nations, confronting Arab and Israeli, is a laudable example—but nothing corrupts more than impotence—or, lacking a central ultimate weapon, an executive world government, which, if defied, could spell a world at war. Is this then the way?

Emphatically, as Sir Alec Douglas-Home has said, we need "a conceptual framework". A new political formation, which indeed, unless it is merely "a détour" through international dreams, is indeed an epoch-making change, which will primarily be held together by the cement of mutual confidence and trust, established over years. But this sentiment has to take official shape as a choice and approval of particular guide-lines directed towards clear goals.

The Atlantic Treaty Alliance indeed, whatever is done in the economic sphere, can itself provide the design, at least for Britain, of the political community of the future with its strategic plans. A political community which excluded North America is basically undesirable for Britain, whatever may be the position for France. Whether a permanent dichotomy between the political-strategic and the fiscal-economic communities is practicable or emotionally sufferable is another question.

Further, the principle of conduct for which, in 1940, I chose the phrase "organic consultation" requires institutionalization in appropriate channels, an infrastructure of accepted, even if informal, channels as distinct from those of the routine diplomacy of foreign affairs.

The pluralist American Constitutional structure does not make this easier. There have been justifiable complaints that, difficult and maybe undesirable although an official common policy for N.W. Europe may be—which depends upon whether the unity is one of genuine like-mindedness or of resented bargain and compromise—even where with the United States there may be likemindedness, the machinery of accord is lacking or inadequate and too departmentalised. There is nothing which one might call an Atlantic secretariat. The infrastructure of unity is indispensable. Henry Kissinger's new "Charter of the Second Period" may stimulate its provision.

One may yet suspect a deeper and less mechanical, a more deep-rooted, difficulty. There may be, not one political formation growing but, however strenuously denied, two— and it is our fate to choose between these rival frameworks. There is the organization springing from the former desire of the late 'Forties for a close fusion, even Carolingian, between defeated ex-enemy countries, German and Italy, and a France only recently Vichy-shaped (much of its Resistance Communist). This formation was anti-Hitler, European Continental in inception and view, to a significant measure Catholic-confessional in its first phase. From this, in direct line of succession, comes the faith in a like-minded "European Community" yet to be born. Churchill was its godfather, but his view was more global. Like Churchill, one may see the beneficial possibilities of this Union of the Defeated. It shows adaptability. It could end the Franco-German feud. But, also like Churchill, I could confess to something short of a total spiritual commitment to what omits most of the history of my own country and hands away its advantages. My name for this handover, if *taken out of the earlier context, is betrayal.*

In the cynical sense that it pays to be defeated, one can note that Britain today is, if lucky, equated in prestige with Japan although Britain is enchained, at Brussels and thanks to the Heath policy, as one ninth of the European union, whereas Japan is now reckoned by its champions to have the same weight as the total mass of Europe—an ironic conclusion of what was for Japan, a fortunate defeat. It is not inappropriate in such a political context to declare that the time has come for somebody "to speak for Britain".

Quite different was the earlier framework of the Atlantic Treaty Powers, as they later became. These were the victorious Powers of the 1939-45 war, non-Continental in nucleus, with their own like-minded Community, to be called the "Atlantic Community", with its historical Anglo-Saxon nucleus or germ but including a re-shaping Commonwealth of thirty-two countries, emphatically inter-racial and international. The European and the Atlantic Community were not the same. Commonwealth relations made this clear. The Atlantic Community, as a concept and a fact shaping conduct in peace and war, was the earlier formation. However, the European Community, for its own interest, strength and purposes, came to stress the importance of including Britain but certainly not the Commonwealth. Even France, which had moved *out* of NATO, in the end thought that it could be advantageous if Britain moved *in* to EEC (although never as any Anglo-Saxon "Trojan horse"). Whatever Hitler had regarded as a fact—Anglo-American effective unity— now became regarded as a danger.

There was the clear risk—and in 1973 this is an appreciated risk—that the whole N.W. "European Community" could develop only as a sad white elephant, an ill-articulated Leviathan, a Customs Union, never fully completed. It must yet be re-emphasised that there is no original and no intrinsic reason whatsoever why, the European Community being neither the root nor framework of the Atlantic one, but an experimental prototype of how the other and earlier Community might shape, there should be antagonism between the smaller community and the larger, any more than between the Commonwealth and the older historic States. But, within the U.N., the larger Atlantic Community was the farthest stage that one could go practically towards an executive world organisation, especially if the *bonanza* of *détente* could be added.

France, in the larger Community, whatever the desire for

amity and functional parity, could not expect to occupy the still massive position of America—save maybe in alliance with the U.S.S.R. or as spokesman, along with China, for all the Middle Powers. However, in N.W. Europe the problem was, once France was authentically in the Atlantic Community, could it expect any influence greater than that of Germany, an influence it had a great chance of possessing in an exclusive Western Europe, despite defence costs.

The position of Britain, unlike that of the Continental countries, was unique. Clearly a member, indeed a founder member, of the larger, earlier community, it was yet strategically and, world free trade apart, economically involved with the smaller. The newer Community of the "friends in defeat" could be French led, which the older Community of the First and maybe of the Second, Atlantic Charter could never be!

The task of those who frame a necessary Second Charter, which will come to terms with a very deep diversity of aims, is not just to recite inoffensive pieties but to emphasise the need for an open community (such as the Commonwealth once was, however weak), sufficiently like-minded to obtain consensus and with mutual confidence organized to respect the majority will, the rule of international law, for mutual consultation—even by the Americans—not for incipient dominance in the balance of interests. Here German, if not French, support may be expected.

In brief, what is required is a Charter which accepts what Kissinger himself has chosen to call an "Atlantic Commonwealth", with the co-operative facilities at all levels which might be expected in such a Commonwealth, but not the pretentious ambitions of an aspiring "Fourth Super Power". These birth pangs in developing a new "power-child" are painful but also unnecessary. They promote pride, but not peace. Now is the crucial occasion to make an advance. Further, if events of human misjudgment in Washington cripple American foreign policy amid domestic feuding, it is arguable that it will not be—as was expected—America that will take over global responsibilities from Britain, but a firm new British foreign policy that will take over the affirmation of the new plan.

According to *Newsweek* (August, 1973) the Quai d'Orsay has undermined President Nixon's "Year of Europe" and maybe has prevented him visiting the European Continent in 1973, at least in the expectation of achieving anything. The explanation is not difficult. An Atlantic Conference, as planned, would upset the continuous French plan for European conferences designed to confirm the economic and diplomatic strength of the Paris-centred French position in Europe and, indeed, in world diplomacy.

> "For the past three months the French have used all their considerable diplomatic finesse to undermine President Nixon's Year-of-Europe."

The conclusion of this diplomatic (but divisive) finesse may be that, before the end of the century, France may be begging, as Attlee said, her friends to rescue her.

It may be added that some American Pressmen and politicians have stoutly contributed to the same cause, blandly refusing to recognise that, however pleasing a domestic campaign of scandal may be, the diminution of the personal influence of Richard Nixon at this moment is the diminution in fact of the international influence of the President and of the Presidency, and that this diminution means for this decade the demolition of the influence of America herself. The time is coming when the American people, aroused from its latest Watergate obsession, will turn on the *New York Times* and *Washington Post*, take their measure and maybe rend them.

If the appeal is to "the democratic will of the people", then the answer is that the people have, as I have said, spat in their face by electing, on a landslide, the man whose policy these papers opposed and by subsequent polls affirming, by up to a 70% majority, that 'the people" did not want Nixon—high-handed and "tricky" although his methods may have been and himself no Moses—to be removed from office, even at the bidding of a self-appointed and undemocratic élite of capitalist owners and salaried pundits. Perhaps the most eminent commentator on the Presidency is Theodore H. White, author of a series on "The Making of the President". He writes that it "would be no less than a national tragedy if [the Press] attempted to reverse the verdict of the people at the polls on the technicalities" of a forced entry by government agents, in (as with Mr. Anthony Lewis) "a spasm of morality approaching the hysterical". To which we may add: and a fanatical partisanship often intolerably self-righteous, as the *Times* own correspondent, William Safire, demonstrated in an article of 4th August. The President's agents indubitably broke the law. But so did the F.B.I. agents without legal challenge from the days of Franklin Roosevelt and then of Lyndon Johnson and until such actions were checked in 1966—by Edgar Hoover . . .

In this present age, in coping with executive problems, American law itself might with advantage be changed and brought in closer conformity with practice found tolerable under British law, which can still allow the detention, in emergency, of suspects without trial or appeal. For the rest, the world public is concerned with world power and peace. It is bored stiff with the repeated American preachings, by lawyers and journalists, about ideal morality, not conspicuously observed in America or elsewhere. To ask a journalist to keep his mouth shut may be to ask for a miracle. It is to take away his bread. Nevertheless political maturity includes knowing when to overlook, and when to maintain silence.

Newsweek continues, concerning the Year-of-Europe (which may only serve to display the nastiness of Europe): —

> "It may not be quite dead yet, but the French have reduced it to a dwarf-like parody of the "Grand Design" unveiled by Dr. Kissinger last April. While maintaining every appearance of good diplomatic manners, the French are exceedingly pleased at this point with their performance.

> "Deeply suspicious of the sudden surge of American interest in Europe, the French tried to head off the Year-of-Europe before it ever got started . . . and so with less than five months remaining the French have virtually insured that President Nixon is not going to get an Atlantic Super-Summit or a declaration of Atlantic principles this year."

Meanwhile French policy will be to develop EEC along the lines advantageous to themselves, while announcing that matters unpleasant for them, such as CAP, should be declared "non-negotiable", under threat that France herself may move out. The reply must surely be that, in this event, France herself is 'non-negotiable" and that Gaullist politicians and diplomats are best left, as the Psalmist says, to fall into a pit of their own digging and to strangle themselves with their own manipulations. France is not going to dominate diplomacy—although, thanks to the French, Moscow well may—and this *without détente*.

In his speech of 2nd August, to the International Platform Association in Washington, Henry Kissinger pleaded for a bipartisan and indeed non-party foreign policy.

> "There can be no moratorium in the quest for a peaceful world . . . Especially at this moment of necessary self-examination we must also re-affirm the basis of our national unity . . . our children will not judge us by the magnitude of our ordeal but only by the adequacy of the response."

Unlike the young Heath, whom M. Pompidou then alleged he found to be his sole British supporter in Europe, those who advocate support of EEC *within* the wider framework but nevertheless give all support for the Atlantic Community, and who also advocate a new Atlantic Charter as a statement of its plan, will not find themselves standing alone. It is a plan more confederate than centralised by the Rome Treaty and Brussels Commission. Maybe it is Mr. Heath, advocate of Britain as the Ninth State, who will again find himself standing on his own as out of accord with the British tradition and having lost credibility with his facile promises of British gains.*

I personally feel myself to be under orders both for the purposes of peace and for the welfare of our own people. The potential market of 700 million persons, with small risk of conflict with GATT, within the Atlantic Community, has already been discussed. Strategically the omission of the Latins, whatever may be French policy on NATO, and disregard for the politics of North Africa and of the Mediterranean, however complex, seems to me unrealistic, whatever the difficulties of even an authentic desire for co-operation— a matter, in the Western Mediterranean alone, involving France, Spain, Italy and Malta, the Arab world apart. Nor would I omit specific reference to those organizations, such as the United Nations, so much needing re-invigoration and the discarding of diplomatic hypocrisies, which institutions according to their powers do militate in favour of an internationalism on the horizon—see the Wilson principles and statements alike by Roosevelt and Willkie—and against a chauvinism, ever ready to put on its boots and armbands.

These reservations made, I reiterate the comments, earlier quoted, made to me in Gettysberg in October, 1967, by

* *Vide : For God's Sake, p.423.*

President Dwight Eisenhower. "What I have always wanted to see is a political union, with no holds barred, of the United States, the United Kingdom, Australasia, EFTA and perhaps Germany." (The omissions were very deliberate and put into words which I do not here quote.) The marching order followed: "Keep the idea alive".

This is also what I want. A change may be advisable here and there. But when we come to discuss a Second Atlantic Charter, which purposefuly refers back to the First and which will be opposed bitterly by those who have a smaller game to play, a clear line of paternity runs back from before Willkie and Eisenhower and on to the "Atlantic Commonwealth" concept defended by Dr. Kissinger.

Maybe the British Commonwealth has now been murdered. But maybe—and this depends upon the will of nations and their leadership—the Atlantic Commonwealth will provide us with what peace welcomes as the next step and which we must now take.

At the beginning of this book I indicated the danger of what is called "the Fork in the Road". Even when we are talking in what is called "trilateral terms", the very real dangers are there of admitting a fundamental division between the "European" (which is indeed so little of Europe) and the "American" set-up. It is rather a division to be repudiated and which Britain must repudiate, since it belongs entirely to neither. It is closer to Ottawa than to Brussels or Palermo. This should be pugnaciously asserted.

War hitherto has lain in the normal history of mankind. Once the "war time-table" goes into effect, it is only a bold statesman, prepared to take great risks, who can reverse it. In its first stages, like a disease, its symptoms begin to show almost without being noted. It comes with loss of confidence, increasing suspicion, the start of preventative military precautions. Politicians will follow "the national interest". But realistically, stable peace is a prime factor in even national interests. And those who are critics of that prime interest have to be dealt with without ruth and without compunction about their prestige. The basic and far from easy issue of maintaining world peace may lie heavier in the balance than any issue of personalities, of the incessant party advantage, even of legalities affirmed under one Constitution but not under another, perhaps more recent. The vision of how to execute the great design, the opportunity to seize on the issue, does not come every year, with mediocre politicians of little faith and much cynicism in charge. And the opportunity, once lost, may not recur for a generation. Let us praise God for M. de Talleyrand, who understood a Revolution and gave a century of peace.

A sincere policy of *détente* for human good—with Russia, with China—must be strenuously pursued. Only if it becomes apparent that this policy is merely a sedative, to make more possible some tactical surprise, is it necessary to lead from strength. Such strength will yet not be the quality of any divided and jealous West. It is a quality which demands a united Atlantic Community, united in consensus, where so long as national States remain no one yet claims to be master. If here we fail, we prepare the Third World War.

VI

In Summary*

As our contemptibly little planet or human prison spins on its way through the universe problems arise which we, cousins of the anthropoid ape—we whom Swift called the Yahoos and Shakespeare called Calibans—endeavour to answer or meet present disaster. Less dignified than the lion and less loyal than the dog, we yet boast as our own both a comprehension of reason and an aesthetic sense that seems, if not unique since the birds may have it, at least uniquely developed. "Our" universe and all the stars may be seen as some gigantic and divine time-clock, harmonious in its parts. Or again these stars and our small planets may be analysed as a matter for a divine croupier or as no more than innumerable gas-jets, in all far more closely giving us a vision of Dante's Hell than of God's Paradise. Lost in this world we have to develop our philosophy; find our guide lines; make our choices.

In the human and political sphere we are confronted with the need for this moral guideline in the labyrinth, even though, deserting what Lord Russell told them was their traditional obligation to wisdom, the most fashionable school of our contemporary philosophers, like the Schoolmen in their late decadence, with Socrates put questions but excuse themselves from answering them. Like the mediaeval Spanish logician, Raymond Lull, who was the father of the computer, they play chess with words. Unfortunately, where they could be useful analysts, they too seldom analyse the verbal superstitions and ambiguities which infect the study of politics— words used uncritically about sovereignty, authority, conservatism, liberty for all, equality from birth. However, it

* The present chapter, added after the rest of the book was printed, endeavours to bring up to date discussion in the spring of 1974 and subsequent to Mr. Secretary Kissinger's London speech of 12 December 1973, first suggested by the author, and to correspondence of 12 October 1972—January 1974 between Dr. Kissinger and the author. This chapter was delivered as an address at Yale University on 7 May 1974.

may be best not to answer the critical and verbal conundrums but to seek to solve practical problems.

The least controversial criterion about action would seem to be whether that action contributes to the accepted good of humanity. That humanity has indeed, in a recognizable if pigmy form, been about for around two and a half or three million years. With medium luck we can expect it to endure for another million or so. This million years—or shall we say, more modestly, this next thousand years—provides us with a time scale.

Before we go further, we should note that what an expert or indeed any reasonable man would judge, e.g., in the case of limited raw material, is needful for human good in the long run is by no means necessarily the same as that which a democratic majority, at any given place or time, may judge will most contribute to their short-range individual comfort, pleasures or pursuit of happiness. As Aristotle said: "Desire has no limits". The majority that wants fast cars—"one for each of the family"—wants it now, whatever the Shah of Persia may say about future solar energy. What yet matters is the good of the race—of humanity. A government has to assess the respective claims; and to appeal, if it can, to rational foresight against private emotion.

It has been said, not only by M. Mendès-France (Aneurin Bevan said the same), that *gouverner c'est choisir*. The problems, even of an eminent kind, of civilization are innumerable. Nevertheless, four are prominent: "the Four P's"—those of Poverty, Population, Pollution, and Peace. It is here argued that the Peace, War and Conflict issue should be given priority of attention; and I so argued in my vice-presidential address, *Pax Mundi,* at the Rome Conference of the World Academy of Art and Science.

Poverty is an immemorial problem but it is also a relative one. There are indeed objective tests, as in the "Plimsoll Line" Test of inadequate nutrition. But, as Ghandi explained to the Lancashire unemployed of the "Thirties", what for Lancashire was poverty for many in India was opulence. There is no level of living which cannot set up standards, such that what was regarded as a luxury does not come to be regarded as a necessity.

Likewise, when, thanks to growth of population, demand for example in food, industrial facilities and amenities, outdistances supply, the poverty of the poor becomes more conspicuous. Nevertheless, the population problem is not susceptible to cure by some ready formula. The voice of Nature and of instinct, which fortunately impels so many of the race of lemmings periodically to drown themselves, does not speak to human kind . . . The rate of increase of population, as the standard of living rises, e.g. in Algeria, may be frightening— what President Boumedienne calls "the Arab bomb" which, for a second time in history, could insure Arab dominion. It is critical that the command given to Abraham, as leader of a small nomadic tribe, today nearly four thousand years on faces entirely new technological conditions. But there are underpopulated lands such as Australia, still waiting (maybe for Catholics to fill them); or, again, lands such as China which are only over-populated on the assumption that vast areas not only are not arable but must remain non-arable.

One problem to prevent contraception or sterilization being opted for first, if it is to be voluntary, in an anti-eugenic sense by those who should adopt it last and least. The issue is a controversial one of freedom of choice. It may be one of discriminating taxation or for the elimination of violence. Incidentally, it is the tiger and not the deer who has to be statutorily protected from violence. For the moment it is not one that unites humanity in some urgent vision of an instant common goal.

Among politicians it is almost as acceptable to preach hatred of pollution and "love of the earth" in conservation, as to preach love of one's mother, although the electoral acceptability of this campaign and of that against wastage of limited materials is quite remarkably recent, the spoliation of nature being, until the other day, rather regarded as an outward and visible sign of progress in industrial enterprise. More than the population problem, the pollution issue invites legislation and compulsion. The industrial effluent of individual enterprises in one country can pollute the waters of a lake, such as Erie, which wash the shores of another. Some remedies, suggested or planned, would seem more compatible with a socialist or even communist philosophy than with any ideology of strictly individualist enterprise. But, for this very reason, issues of freedom arise which make many of the more obvious remedies highly controversial.

Again, if there were no population, there would be no energy problem. And, if there were too much energy supply there would be more widespread pollution. Energy is a derivative problem—"energy for what?"

However, if the world problems of population and of pollution are both highly controversial and also of recent popular recognition, like the old problem of what to do about acute poverty the equally ancient problem of how to end war and produce stable peace demands preeminent attention. It is not novel but rallies a wide consensus that an agreed goal of peace has to be achieved. The question is: How?

The peculiarity, then, of the Peace Problem is the remarkable degree of human consensus to the effect that stable Peace is a major (and may be, at this present, *the* major) human public goal. Those who claim today that "warfare is a remedy for mankind diseased" are few: and those for whom "the war-game" is immemorial are primitive. It cannot even be claimed that modern war is eugenic in individual terms. Perhaps the only recent issue on which there has been like unanimity of purpose has been the Abolition of Slavery. Here, however, there is the sobering reflection that, largely, slavery was abolished by war.

How, then, shall we abolish war? Almost two centuries ago the philosopher Immanuel Kant wrote his plea for *Ewige Friede,* "Lasting Peace" (1795). The goal was acclaimed as admirable by all, acceptable by most. The mistake is to suppose that the means to it are easy to achieve. All history proclaims the contrary. It may be, as Hobbes thought, that to produce and enforce peace one requires a deterrent terror. Maybe a new technology can provide it. Thanks to artillery the king, in the late Middle Ages, won against the free barons. Does the hydrogen bomb itself provide, against human egotism, the requisite terror to reenforce reason—provide the ultimate weapon?

As distinct from "contingent pacifism"—"my right to decide for myself what wars I will not engage in"—absolute pacifism on principle has the merit of providing for the war problem a happily simple answer. "If you don't want wars, don't fight them". After all, the anarchists say, all human beings are naturally good except when they are members of that minority of them who are naturally bad. Unhappily, however, it is just this minority, and those whom they can control, who constitute the core of the problem. Should we meet Hitler or Stalin with folded arms? Shall we bring in Stalin against Hitler? As I know from personal conversation,

Gandhi himself was not an absolute pacifist.* For peace a peace-minded public is indeed requisite. But no police? As the Mahatma stated, granted a decision of an international impartial tribunal, recommending police action, he would support such action. What he doubted was the probability of impartiality.

The major modification of the absolute pacifist position, religious or otherwise, is that adopted from the Fourth Century by Catholic and other Christian churches. Christians may only fight in "just wars", such as those of self-defence or for some major cause of social justice. The trouble is that for many years groups of international lawyers have been trying to arrive at precise definitions of "aggression" and "self-defence" and have not yet succeeded. No other than the late head of the Roman Holy Office expressed a doubt whether any war in the contemporary world, the protagonists lacking or declining an international tribunal, could indeed be just. The appeal to some subjective sense of justice, where each man indignantly claims to be both judge and jury in his own case, leads only to anarchy or force. Merit lies in the flat declaration of Kant that "justice" does not exist save where there is a proper assize, a competent tribunal and a "common external authority". Once again we have to ask: But how do we get this? Is that vague thing called "World Public Opinion" to be enough, as it seemingly was for Mr. Secretary Kellogg?

Or shall we rather turn to the precision of "The Rule of Law"? The incisive comment of President Andrew Jackson on a decision of Chief Justice John Marshall is generally here ignored. "John Marshall has delivered his judgment: now let him enforce it". The stress of the argument is clear. Unless we put our instant trust for the enforcement of peace in the flatulence of the United Nations, with its hundred and more "sovereign states", then we would seem to need a world executive or government. Centuries ago this was praised by Dante in the days of the Holy Roman Empire. If this indeed were the goal, what has come nearest to it?

The Celestial Emperor of China? I do not see (like the Chinese although I may) the world as being as yet ruled, despite population distribution, by a new Chinese empire— although, balanced against the Soviets, there may be a case. The *Pax Britannica*, chiefly naval in its executive force and

* *Vide* G. Catlin: *In the Path of Mahatma Gandhi.*

tolerated because usually the champion of Free Trade? Or shall we re-establish the *Pax Romana,* maintained as Justinian said by law and arms? Asked in what period in the world's history he would rather have chosen to live, one of the greatest of historians, Edward Gibbon, replied: In the days of the Adoptionist Emperors—in the days of the Emperor Hadrian. Is then restoration of the Roman Empire on a world scale what world politics requires? Or can the champions of democracy offer something better? Should the Super-powers aim to repress the disproportionate claims of second or third rate Powers, left-overs of an earlier world?

Or should we seek a solution for our problem by adding on more "demi-super Powers": USA; USSR; a further Western Empire led by France; Japan; maybe Brazil. Certainly it is naïve if those who argue for multipolarity be caught out overlooking the centuries of the Arab Empire (including the sect of the Assassins in Syria) which extended to Spain and even to France, followed by an Islamic Empire which threatened Vienna nearly three centuries ago and which has now—for technological reasons, as Britain for reasons of coal and textiles before it—blossomed anew. Or should we multiply Super-Powers yet more—the "Impotent Powers" so that, quarrelling and undecided, they end, after sixty years, yet again in what Lowes Dickenson called "the International Anarchy".

The more the Super-Powers, the less the Law; and the less the executive force, the more its disputes. The more any state in isolation exalts *la Gloire*—its own—the more it invites its own repression.

The generally accepted answer here sanctioned under the United Nations Charter is that, granted the appropriate supra-national institutions, peace can be maintained "regionally". The problem is to maintain détente between the Regions. As the disgruntled Tacitus wrote of the Roman peace: "They make a desolation and they call it peace". Perhaps we can do better*.

ii

The first principle in Economics is the balance between demand, supply and costs. What is not equally recognized

---

* The attention of the reader is here called to Francis Wilcox and W. F. Haviland (edit), *The Atlantic Community, a Complex Imbalance,* 1969, and R. B. Manderson Jones's *The Special Relationship,* 1972.

(although political scientists have been at some pains to point it out) is that the first principle of Political Science is, if demands for political goods such as peace and concord are to be met, then these goods do not come down from some democratic heaven or from unusual good will, but involve costs. What costs then—unpleasant, soaring costs—are we prepared to pay?

What can we, even under treaty, safely give up which may seem to endanger our local security and the local traditions of life. In emotional times all such erosion of sovereignty may seem to be "endangering our national life". Would then a Federation of Israel, Amman and Lebanon endanger the life of the parts? Have Scotland and Virginia, by sacrificing sovereignty, been only losers? Does an Ulster Orangeman think he has sacrificed his birthright by union with Britain rather than upholding it by a union upon which he insists, like Mrs. Micawber, whether Britain wants it or not?

After the days of Danton's National army and the French Revolution Nationalism passed, like a cholera plague, over Europe to lose itself in Asia and Africa. Now the symptoms, deadly to internationalism, seem to be showing again in Europe as a new tribalist chauvinism. Lethal to peace, opposition to it is not to be confused with something radically different—opposition to a decent local loyalty to family, village, and country, which is a cement of patriotic life and, as Rousseau for once rightly said, by giving a sense of "belonging", is "a major source of civic virtue".

The significance of sovereignty was acclaimed by Blackstone as a power-absolute. As that great man, Australian born, the late Professor Sir Gilbert Murray wrote, fusions of sovereignty are far more feasible when there is a "sharing of values" rooted in history, unlike the present situation of states running around like headless chickens, in search of a new nest in which they may be warm. Patriotism, even of the village, is to be unambiguously praised by social man as is also the family; but internationalism and the pride of the world citizen, as with Goethe, is to be praised also.

It is sometimes stated, as a self-evident qualification in folk wisdom, that all states—and maybe all people—are motivated by self-interest. Professor Hans Morgenthau risks this proposition. In the words of a philosophic tag, "it all depends upon what you mean". What *is* the substantial self-interest of a people? War? An imperialism (more from Manchester than from Rome) exploiting economically your neighbour? There is political astigmatism in construing "national interest" in a fashion more material and short-ranged than any prudent man would construe his own personal interest in taking out insurance policies. To be blind to danger and to be astigmatic on policies to ones advantage are different things.

However, as said earlier, a variant of Regionalism has recently been proposed, most eminently by the sometime Director of the Institute of Strategic Studies, London, Professor Alistair Buchan, which would seem to combine the animus of nationalism (maybe with some geopolitical support) with the cold and more calculated aspects of internationalism. It is called "Multi-polarity" and is stated in conscious reaction against the possible Bi-polarity of the Super-Powers. Instead of this it visualizes maybe five or more "Great Powers", a united N.W. Europe being one. It is a proposal which, if not interesting Slavic Europe or the Swedes, Swiss, Spaniards and the rest, nevertheless interests N.W. Europeans. Is not this Multi-polarity something more reliable for peace than a perhaps deceptive détente? (Or, on the contrary, from Moscow to San Francisco, from Cairo to Tehran, do we not rather see the European Epoch as ending for the first time since Marathon and, along with this, see the eclipse of France?)

As Mr. Melvin Laird, sometime U.S. Secretary of Defence, writes (*Readers Digest*, Feb. 1974): "Will détente signal an era of real cooperation?" From the days of Lenin to those of Stalin, although it was frequently proclaimed that there had never been conflict in arms, the ideological difference between the USA and the USSR was almost total. From the days of the Polish "free election" issue in 1945 until the other day the prevailing ideology was that of Cold War. To change that relation, doctrinally inculcated for a period of over fifty years, into one of détente cannot be a job of facile opportunism, even if we may agree that pragmatic détente and a "real cooperation" on values may be different things.

On the contrary, if Mr. Secretary Kissinger wishes to unite more closely than heretofore the Atlantic area into a true community *and*, at the same time, to achieve détente with the communist Eastern area, his task can only be described as titanic and on the same level of diplomatic accomplishment as that of Metternich, Castlereagh and Talleyrand at the Congress of Vienna, which gave us, not rhetoric, but peace for a hundred years. The task is not just to give the American electorate, through the popular media, elementary instruction in diplomacy and foreign affairs on the Wilsonian "fish bowl" model, beloved by ambitious journalists with a reputation to make, but to achieve actual, effective peace. The effort will require support from the American electorate of proportionate titanic magnitude, intolerant of mere carping and, hopefully, of a more solid judgment than it has always displayed in the election of its own representatives.

The first thing the electorate has to do is to confront the technicalities with humility—difficulties intrinsic to the diplomatic task. With no history, prior to this century, of major concern with international affairs, the United States is inclined to put domestic politics ahead of international affairs. The United States is inclined to put domestic politics ahead of international judgement and, as George Kennan was to complain, is inclined first to moralize on "the dubious politics of foreigners" and then to be "disillusioned".

American history until the beginning of this century has been domestically preoccupied and with an inclination to view with contempt the tough realities of foreign affairs, just as Whig philosophy, from which the American Constitution sprang, was pervaded by distrust of all executive power which did not conform with the views of the legislature. For the Whigs the less executive power the better.

It was sentimentally laudable for European nations "to join up", even if this chanced to put into the foreground of integration those who had been joined together in the opponent leadership of the last war—Germany, Italy and the supporters of the official Vichy government. As Mr. Heath said, by an unfortunate lapse, the aims here of Napoleon and of Hitler were warrantable, provided that means more civilized and less military were adopted than by Emperor and Führer. In a militant Russia they all had a common enemy. And it is a common enemy which unites. (Less was heard in the United States of this logic of union when a possible federal union came nearer home—to Canada and the United States. Why not a "free Quebec" and a union of the rest?)

The integration of Europe—even of a Europe which did not include the Slavic nations or Sweden or the Hispanic Peninsula or Switzerland—can be an approved and desirable goal. But it is only such if this union and community are unambiguously within the framework and wider community of an open Atlanticism, wider even than the Old Commonwealth. The basic issue is not whether (a) the E.E.C. should be accepted on principle; (b) nor whether this organization should be advanced from an economic unification, functionalized or not, to some confederate political union; (c) but whether simultaneously this E.E.C. should be integrated, as of lesser importance, with a confederated Atlantic Community, as of major importance, with not only strategic but also with economic, political and cultural elements.

That, the Treaty of Rome having been signed, there is no legal power for Britain to insist upon the above diplomatic understanding is doubly inaccurate. No other than General de Gaulle, after his second accession to power, despite acceptance of the Treaty, gave a fundamentally new, and non-federal, interpretation of its meaning, as not *union de l'Europe* but as only *union des patries,* in which France could stand *seul.*

Further, as a matter of the formal legalities, it is no other than the highest British legal authority, Lord Chancellor Hailsham, who has said, in a debate on the E.E.C. Entry, that there were no question of one British government's signatures on atreaty binding on the matter its successor. It could reject the Heath pledges if it so willed or those, for that matter, of Mr. Roy Jenkins or any other—something which pro-E.E.C. journalists have steadily muffled. If the British should prefer to move as closely with the Americans and Australians as with the French they are entirely free to do so—or to move as much in with NATO as, the French Gaullists, including M. Jobert, might choose to move out.

For the present, and with the issue of principle borne well in mind, America should be very chary of believing that the majority of British voters regard themselves or would wish to regard themselves as more European "continentals" than as members of the Commonwealth. Moreover, in the words of President Truman to me, "Let us be honest: there is a special interest, isn't there?" And likewise between America and parts of Europe, such as Germany, there may be, for special purposes as Mr. Kissinger has said, a special interest.

Were, however, the European portion of the Atlantic Community to be so defined as to be in rivalry and indeed potential opposition to the rest, seven or nine nations in a Pirandello quest, consulting the psychotherapists about their non-existent "identity", the result for peace might not be so good. It might be not only guilty of a "continentalist" heresy, but profoundly objectionable. Culturally, strategically, politically, even economically, it could be a disaster for peace.

The immediate post-war policy, contrary in emphasis to that of Eden, and indeed of Attlee and Wilson, that Britain should be "pushed into Europe", is intelligible indeed in view of the situation. In a Cold War epoch it was natural that Mr. Dean Acheson should be impatient if Britain, going beyond Ernest Bevin's supporting commitment in WEU, did not rally to a united plan against Soviet expansionism, not least in Germany (although unexpectedly, on Berlin, it was Aneurin Bevan who responded with emphasis to the challenge).

It was also not unexpected that John Foster Dulles, concentrating on his S.E. Asia policy of confrontation and on his alliances, resented it that "Europe", including Britain, did not unite in an integral resistance to Soviet expansion in the West, thereby failing to relieve the American tax-payer and drafted soldier of a burden which could be avoided if "Europe would stand on its own feet". What both Dulles— although certainly not Eisenhower in policy as stated to me and already quoted—and the European enthusiasts failed to take into account was the possibility of a Europe, with a new pumped-up semi-Super-Power "identity", wanting to use its new power to object to American policy itself. Not unnaturally there has been since those days and had to be a fundamental change—not from the policy for America indicated by Eisenhower and by both the Roosevelts, but from that of the epoch of an America in President Nixon's word "obsessed" by Asian policy in the Pacific and by the "cold war", especially there.

An integration of N.W. Europe, going beyond a Customs Union or continental commercial arrangement for banks and particular industries, a system for keeping up farm rates and stretching on to a common policy which does but substitute for the national egotism of a people the continental egotism of an area, can become insufferable and inimical to world peace. This Gaullism has little in common with the earlier pro-Atlanticist European Movement. Instead of the European Movement being the European stage or "first stage" (as some hoped) of Atlanticism—and so recited by Lord Harlech —the Atlantic is being widened by what is clearly a French "continental initiative". The exclusive dream of a Hallstein, however French modified, is not over but it has diverged significantly from the pro-American one of a Monnet.

It is not the "Common Market", but the unreal Gaullist

concept of a "European Europe", with an "adversary identity" of the Six or Nine, which has to be condemned. Behind this lurks the idea of a "Personality" or "Identity", itself entirely real, of a France whose "national interest" M. Jobert is dedicated to defend. Europe is to be a field for French diplomacy, because the Western Atlantic Powers were "not European". But France was not to be excluded from Middle Eastern negotiations, in which the Soviet Union was militarily concerned, because France had ancient historic interests in the Middle East (as also from Quebec to South East Asia). If excluded, then there must be a conference of oil-producing countries and of a United Europe, to which North America could not be invited.

In the words of *Het Parool*, Amsterdam (Feb. 15, 1974), as to a global integrated approach "the Eight might begin considering to try it without France". A new world energy order may be required, in which the Arabs and not least the Shah can be invited to participate. A new Project Interdependence. The same thought was put forward at the time of the Washington Oil Conference by a member of the Department of State: "if some people are going to go around poisoning all the wells, that is not the kind of company we would wish to keep". It is not easy to hold together a European Conference assembled to agree, so "united" that each would demonstrate European unity by each following his own national interest. As between Britain and France there is no point in polite future pretentions of harmony where there is no harmony and, on the French premises, there can be none. Here Edward Heath is merely maverick to the public opinion of his own country.

One understands the chagrin at interference with the immemorable dream of a European culture shaped by Paris, and of a continental diplomacy still, after three centuries, dominated by her. The resentment is not diminished when France's aspiration of a "European Europe" is accepted for the Nine in a "European Region", and then—in Syria, South East Asia, Quebec—France is told that the heirs of Louis XIV should keep to their own portion of Europe, her language less widely distributed than that of Spain; and that she should not thrust her presence into areas not in the N.W. European Region or demand a seat at every negotiation of the Super-Powers, where she is militarily dependent on America.

The issue has been one, not of military dominance, but for diplomatic precedence. Since 1945, the British have been advised to "cut themselves down to size". This they have done with almost alarming speed. Inside Europe or outside, the Commonwealth neglected, they have achieved the status of "an off-shore island".

In terms of the Continent of Europe France has better maintained its position. The propaganda thesis of M. Ortoli that Britain, "by Entry", has joined the most powerful bloc in the world is grossly deceptive. Precisely this bloc strength is more a future hope than a present achievement; it is not true technically except in limited trade terms; and an Atlantic bloc, with greater population and wealth (and much present trade), would be stronger in terms of British advantage.

Historically, French policy has been, and still remains, to sustain a diplomatic fight for French presidency in Western Europe; to claim that it is for "European Europe" alone and for its Region, not for a trans-Atlantic stranger, to shape what are exclusively European affairs; always, nevertheless, to entertain the possibility that this directorship could be extended to include, "up to the Urals", the Russians, who are also Europeans; but to dance with indignation at the suggestion that the European Powers, being also historically *not* just regional but global Powers, should be ignored in extra-European arrangements, and maybe prevented from having matters both ways.

If there is as yet no common European policy in, e.g. Palestine—as there is not—this for Paris is indeed regrettable. MM. Pompidou and Jobert have yet no intention of cutting themselves down to size—especially so long as Mr. Heath can be counted upon to play satellite. The E.E.C. suits their policy. An Atlantic Community which goes beyond this in essence—or even an effective NATO diplomacy—does not suit it.

An obstinate element in French policy is distrust fed by jealousy. It is a misfortune that France is geographically essential to an effective NATO. As Dean Eugene Rostow has put it, in his extremely important and wise book, *Peace in the Balance,* despite such talk of contributing to Western strength, strategically French policy, by offering the prospect of division, makes a contribution to Western weakness in the name of French claims to independent sovereignty.*

The issue is not one only of the gain for world peace of a strong and united Atlantic Community; but, secondly, of the real gain for peace of a pragmatic USA-USSR *détente*. Here again any startling success of American policy can be as vexatious for M. Pompidou's successor as for M. Jobert. Such success challenges the "identity of Europe" and the exclusive club of Europeans (N.W.) as representing special interests, not for the world, but as distinct from and even against the world—except, of course, in so far as, e.g., France has had its own global historic interests, all over the world from Quebec to Syria and Annam.

iii

The Dutch Press has recently pointed out the unique advantage to the United States in having as Secretary of State someone for whom there is, with all respect to Acheson and Marshall, no precedent in the list of American Secretaries and to whom there is unlikely to be an early equal successor—a man not only of wide and technical European experience but by birth in contact with the Old World Mind. However to such brilliance, imagination and sound judgment, expressed in a head-on attack on the problems in S.E. Asia, China, Russia, the Middle East and Europe, there is a corrollary which requires no Rochefoucauld to underline: the intense jealousy of others, both these whose own pettier plans he upsets and the conceited and arrogant men at home who, although they are not diplomats, think they were born to do better in diplomacy than their neighbours, and the war-mongering, notoriety seeking cartoonists.

* Eugene V. Rostow (*Peace in the Balance*, Simon and Schuster, 1972, pp. 339-40) speaks of the so-called "dumb-bell theory" of Atlantic relations, "which theory contends that alliance relationships should be loosened so that Western Europe and Japan . . . could operate in world politics in their own orbits, allied to the United States, but independent of it too. Under those circumstances there would be four major centres of power . . . Their orbits in world politics would be harmonies, and collisions avoided, these men argue, by a Gaullist law of celestial gravitation, upon which we could safely rely to maintain equilibrium. As a matter both of fact and of theory, this view was a fantasy . . . In any case there is no way in which Western Europe could soon become an effective political entity."

That politician who affirms with vigour that his chief concern is world peace, and this is more than some "gossamer dream", but who also regards any practical step of "détente" as destined to fail, is unimpressive as a statesman. The cause being adequate, as ending war is, one has to take some calculated risks. Mainly one has to be shrewdly aware of what ones armaments can achieve.

The excellently timed message to President Nixon from Mr. Brezhnev who (Jan. 30) lauded the Russian-American détente, at a delicate point in his journey to see Castro before his visit to America, can be dismissed, by those who so choose, as deception. Likewise one can dismiss as "unreal" Brezhnev's statement in Cuba that revolutions are not for export; and, as without significance, Khruschev's memorable comment that one cannot build a new civilization on a heap of radioactive ash. Or the Chinese, in damning the "Russian imperialists". But politics cannot be shaped by subjective prejudice. Objectively, Communism is not monolithic, as Dulles inclined to hold; and the Politit bureau is not monolithic either. One can choose to run risks with Brezhnev or, Brezhnev ousted, one can await the confrontation of Schlesinger and Grechko.

We can divide the enemies of Secretary Kissinger's policy, here called the Wreckers, into two groups, foreign and domestic. The policy of the first can be well illustrated by a group of politicians abroad who would certainly declare that, while opposing the Communist Party at home, they could yet be all in favour of détente with the Soviet Union abroad—but *not* a Russian-American détente which could spell in their eyes an alien condominium and a new world imperialism.

To take a particular case, the present government of France is certainly not favourable to the large French Communist Party. But, if France cannot expect alone to shape the diplomacy of the entire "Concert of Europe", as conductor, it has always been regarded in the Quai d'Orsai as possible to shape, for effective control as against the German Empire, a détente or entente with Russia. Indeed here was the pre-1914 origin of the Dual Entente. Today a dual entente with Russia could effectively shape Europe, if no better Gaullist policy was available for Europe up to (and beyond) the Urals—and all this with the Americans (and even the Anglo-Saxons) surely left out. Let the British, fortunately by treaty split from the rest of the world, "have their backs against the wall".

However, an effective American-Russian détente, incidentally shaping Europe, could "put paid" to all of this. Hence such a consortium, which could issue, it is felt, in a power-conscious Russia being cold to the flirtations of Paris, is detestable, most "unEuropean" and to be as much obstructed as any Washington-initiated oil consortium. The fundamental objection is that it might actually succeed—and ditch "European Europe" policy. Indeed the alarm could be raised that it might produce a world condominium—even a world peace whose makers had forgotten de Gaulle. It might even produce an American hegemony in the West. Admittedly, for reasons of liberal and Whig history there have been few signs of such hegemony at present—unless it be in nuclear weapons on which (detestable irony) the security and independence of France depends—a dependent independence.

In brief, détente is a good thing but not too much. Not if it upsets the traditional priorities. Kissinger's style of détente is unacceptable. Europe is tightly regional to its advantage; but Europe in its policy must also be as global as before. We can, it is suggested, only advance by going backward to past distributions of power.

Moreover, national security is important in Europe. Hence the Atlantic Treaty is important. But it is also laudable to maintain French sovereign independence, so that France can walk out of NATO—the cost being for others to pay. After all, strategically NATO can't operate without use of France's territory. One unhappy reservation, for French policy, has yet here to be admitted. NATO foresees the USSR as the major threat. Nothing unites like common enemies. But suppose an effective Russian-American détente . . . then the key importance of France, its walkings in and walkings out, would cease much to matter. Indeed, instead of the earlier error of identifying "the Atlantic area", of the Atlantic Charter proposals, with something far more local, the "North Atlantic" geographical area, this Atlantic Community could range beyond these misleading geopolitical limits. The world could carry on to peace on its own. Gaullism and Quai d'Orsai could be trumped. Hence "European Europe's" blessings for détente are more contingent than would superficially appear to be the case.

I have also referred to the internal, domestic and native American Wreckers, chiefly journalists and ideologues. There are indeed others. One finds, to one's surprise that, distrustful of a new policy certainly co-ordinated with the President and Commander in Chief, members of the Joint Chiefs of Staff of the Armed Forces have encouraged leaks on the most private issues of peace negotiations. They were not unaware of the burglary of illicit pieces of information. They were ably encouraged in like cases by the example of such investigative journalists as Mr. Jack Anderson, the worthy and scrupulous successor of Mr. Drew Pearson. The Navy was energetically represented by Yeoman 1st Class, Charles Radford. Public reprimand (not only of the Yeoman) might have been in order. (In a like position in Britain he could have been first imprisoned and, in 1940-5, kept in prison, detained without trial, appeal or compensation, at the Home Secretary's "pleasure".)

The Communist Party and S.W.P. have frequently been investigated. Investigation of the Democratic Party Committee (maybe for papers earlier handed to the Navy) might be more difficult—although the Republican eager ward-boys supplied white tape-tabs, and ones which even the janitor could not fail to observe, to make clear their point of entry in this charade. The tap of Watergate trivia, aided by perjuries, continues to drip—nay, by Senator Ervin was turned on to full volume (until his own committee became a source of leaks to the press against the Senator), after which a new legal court, in the sacred name of legality, put a stopper on the older political legal circus and inquisition.

The lawyers' busily amassed their briefs. One federal judge in California *sub-poena'd* the President to appear in person. According to William Safire, of the *International Herald Tribune* itself (5 March 1974) the prosecution has used a key quotation, bogus and misleading, against the President. The puritan journalists of the *New York Times,* "sea-green incorruptibles", built to Pisgah-heights their reputations while, as a correspondent put it to me, their lowlier colleagues provided entertainment in a serial which could go on for months, with much financial advantage to some involved. There was, in these investigations, what Mr. Joseph Kraft has called "a triumph—notably for the *Washington Post*"—but also a "self-important narcissism" and Phariseeism of which Mr. Kraft is not the least guilty offender himself. The "Fourth Estate", non-elected employees of capitalist business, freely suppressed objectionable letters to the press and continued its decade-long vendetta against U.S. Presidents—against the

Executive—on behalf of a Congress which had achieved little constructive or remarkable in foreign affairs since 1918. One recalls by contrast the days when Lloyd George, using the then novel technique of radio, so successfully knocked out the owner of the *Daily Mail* and *Times,* Lord Northcliffe, that Northcliffe never recovered.

However, to tidy up its charges, the *New York Times* warriors, piously disapproving of illegal administrative leaks, for completeness turned their shafts on Henry Kissinger (who had indeed become intolerant about "leaks for all the people, who all have a right to know") as no less guilty than the President in using "wire-tapping".

All sense of political and legal proportion, alike by press and prosecuted, was lost. Forcible entry by the police would not have been so difficult to get authorized, if the White House sleuths had used elementary common-sense. (Mr. Nixon, however, himself champions privacy for all.) The rumours that, in retaliation for bugged "leaks" from the National Security Council, Dr. Kissinger had been responsible for the counter-bugging of the telephone of Mr. Melvin Laird, then Minister of Defence, alluded to in the *Chicago Sun-Times,* Kissinger denounced (*Herald Tribune,* Jan. 14, 1974) as "a malicious, vicious, outrageous lie."

It is probably not far out to say that the damage done to the American world image by the American Press, pre-occupied with mere Washington scourings, and aided by too many lawyers in search of a brief, is something which it will take all of a half-century to make good. No private righteousness by commercial media, no Phariseeism, can repair the public damage. The world round, Americans are identified with charges recklessly exploited—not with the good-doings of humble, righteous investigative reporters, alert like little dogs to sniff at the roots of every tree.

As to wire-tapping, in France, which is certainly a democracy, it is too frequent to merit notice. In Britain Scotland Yard admits to over a thousand authorized wire-tapping cases a year in the war against crime and sedition. Maybe, in the interest of all, what is required is not so much legal action against wire-tappers but legal action to change, to greater realism, an obsolete law itself. Anyhow the future Secretary of State had the firmness to persist—with discoveries truly more remarkable and unexpected among high officers of state than is likely to be found in some psychiatrists' file-cabinet into which the brisk young men of the White House were looking.

The insatiable Press, however, elated by the hunt for big game was not easily to be satisfied. If the Secretary failed, then he failed. But if he conspicuously succeeded? This was scarcely better. Like the politicians in foreign nations who had themselves done little for peace on the record, the gentleman of the press, who feel that they alone really know better than any Secretary how diplomacy should be conducted, found such hasty success, such unheard of momentum, not in the best taste. A lightening diplomacy (like Bismarck's, for that matter) the wreckers, both domestic and foreign, were sure could not be a successful diplomacy. It was "not done" in the best chanceries; was too peremptory; must "come unstuck".

A resolute policy at once of Atlantic integration and of détente has one further risk, and a grave one, to confront. Earlier I have suggested that the fundamental differences that last between peoples are not differences of ideologies and goals—fierce initially but ending as mere convenient propaganda for this or that side. They are clashes on power and about who shall have the power to carry through his plans. Here are required the techniques of adjustment. Nevertheless a passion of indignation about ideologies, the insensate fury of indignation where every man is his private judge, can wreck all chances of détente.

I recall addressing in New York in 1947 a Polish gathering. I expressed my sympathy with their denunciation of Russian policy. But I added that they must not expect us to restart a World War on their behalf. We may sympathize with some of the views of M. Sakharov, although being the inventor of the Russian atomic bomb, constructed as balance against America, is perhaps rather criminal than laudable.

Mr. Solzhenitsyn may be a poet, a man of considerable eminence in letters, a man of persistent courage, although not always most in agreement with those who praise him most—and saucing his discourse by denunciation of the alleged lies in the Western press. By implication he condemns two hundred and fifty million of his compatriots for cowardice in not condemning the atrocities of the tyrant Stalin. Assuming the truth of his facts, not least during the monstrous purges of the "Thirties", he exposes the moral dishonesty of the European statesmen who continued to flatter

Stalin—about whom we should also read Svetlana's account —in the hope that Stalin would join with them. (The explanation of the hypocrisy can be expressed in one word: "Hitler".) Indeed it is contrary to the very Charter of the United Nations to interfere in the internal affairs—even purges—of other nations.

It is late in the day to grow frantic with protest and one suspects hypocrisy in the denunciation. Why not in 1939-45? Today protest is little more than, "objectively", for a Russian author and his publishers a form of war-mongering against, like it or not, ones own country. And as usual, the irresponsible press and the men of letters itch to "get in on the act". Substantially, "they choose war". When détente can be made effective, while justice remains subjective and not the voice of objective law, they are out to stir the emotions of war.

The *Herald Tribune,* in the war-mongering article, "Sand in the Gears", by G. F. Will (Feb. 23, 1974), states that America has been "gloriously awakened by the Solzhenitsyn drama", and that such a desirable "revived anti-Communist impulse" would be fatal to détente as Henry Kissinger envisions it. One can only comment that, if an East-West (or Russian-American) atomic war occurred, does anyone, other than Mr. Will, think that the citizen mass of the 250 million people of the Soviet Union is going to rise as one man, along with Mr. Gromyko and Pope Paul, on behalf of the *Herald Tribune* and *New York Times,* their publishers and staff, together with eminent money-making literary figures such as Mr. Norman Mailer and Mr. Solzhenitsyn's fellow thinkers?

With Mr. Kissinger we have to say of Solzhenitsyn that he has our publicly announced sympathy. Not only a Christ, not only a Thomas More, but all the millions of unpublicized victims of a Stalin or of a Hitler will have that sympathy also . . . To change the analogy, Alexander Solzhenitsyn is the Colonel Dreyfus of Russia—except thta Dreyfus returned to silence. But we must also say that, with all the prospects of world peace consequent on effective détente, and profound as maybe the differences between the philosophies of a Lenin and a Vanderbilt, we will not imperil a world peace in order to appease our consciences about atrocities we ourselves dishonestly connived at in the past. It may be that the greatest enemy of peace is God-like talk about a theoretical justice which is the prerogative of God and history alone.

What then is the Kissinger policy going to lead to in the end? Although naturally denied by those already deeply committed to blind optimism, anyone of political judgment has, for some time, been able to see the risk of "an adversary confrontation", within the "Atlantic Alliance" (or Atlantic Commonwealth) between the transAtlantic world of America, Canada, even Australia, and a segment of Europe militarily concerned to assert its own separate individuality—a N.W. European isolationism.

They can see that the time may well come when British policy, revising that pursued by Edward Heath, may have to detach Britain, in the very interest of the Atlantic Alliance, not from the Common Market on principle, but from a Gaullist-shaped EEC and from any self-centred European organization which is in effect disruptive of the wider organization. If such a return of British policy to its traditional and secessionist avoidance of one-sided implication in Central Europe is to be avoided, a Kissinger policy of affirmation of the strength of the whole Atlantic Community —and by no means solely against the Russians—has to be reiterated. It has also to carry with it that most elusive of things, Senatorial commitment.

If we accept, as Eisenhower certainly did, as Kissinger with his references to an Atlantic Commonwealth does, and as is here advocated, the full Atlantic Community notion and loyalty to it as having priority—which does not have to spell the constitutional legalism of some full federal union—then there are certain practical consequences.

Over thirty years ago I advocated an "Organic Union" (here in general supported, as a "U.S. War Aim", by Walter Lippmann) which, avoiding rigidity, assumed not only the frequency of "Summit Meetings" but also other frequent meetings, interchange of personnel, coordination of policy down to an administrative level, mutual departmental interlocking, together (which we do not yet have) with an international infrastructure which makes such coordination easy. The specific objectives should be to obtain, not any imposed domination, but an Atlantic Commonwealth consensus such as could rally electoral opinion if put to the test, a majority consensus based alike on interest and on sentiment, on calculation and history, on legislation and on common values, on a common vision and a common infrastructure.

In the post-war decades few measures, even if of limited range, worked better in international practical effect than those expressions of the Functionalist philosophy, specific agencies such as High Authorities for Coal and Steel, Atomic

143

Energy in some aspects, and potentially for Transport and Fishing. Here the proposal made by Mr. Secretary Kissinger in London, on Dec. 12, 1973—for a joint effort to control oil consumption, later to be coordinated with a policy for oil production, as a joint (not bilateral) undertaking: a field in which the United States might be a donor but certainly did not have to be a beggar (like France) from anyone—follows an historic pattern set in Europe earlier and promises realistic results in industrial crises. A like agricultural and monetary procedure seems to be indicated, and a like non-competitive procedure in aid to under-developed lands (which even Arabian lands are for some purposes). The international Oil Conference in Washington of February, 1974, was not, as some of the American Pressmen helpfully saw it, "a flop". On the contrary, it compelled the disclosure of an abrasive French policy and served fascinatingly to embarrass in public M. Jobert's best friends.

However, we can go beyond specific projects to the general enunciation of enduring aims. Such enduring concepts, enunciated, arouse the enthusiasm of the electorate, even if they irritate routine civil servants who can see the dangers in such emotion but who, as *chefs de cabinet,* have enunciated few original ideas themselves.

The Atlantic Charter, subscribed to in Placentia Bay off Newfoundland, was of this character, although its moral emphasis was perhaps not re-enforced by the later signature of a major disbeliever, Joseph Stalin—indicating thereby the "open nature" of the concept although it may. Signature has not spelled or implied the condemnation of those who, while co-existent, do not share its views. The Charter has served to emphasize the desirability of a common policy in a specific area, wider than Europe, of those who do. What it does, alike in the Old Charter and in the projected New Atlantic Charter, is to provide guide lines for integration and internationalism, short of the super-regional area of the United Nations Charter but wider than the older national ones.

For such guide lines, indicating both the practical present and the horizon ideals, both policy and institutional structure, the need is today clear in yet another interim period of history. They can show where, for the *pax mundi,* the stepping stones should be placed. Any statesman who makes his life contribution here merits the praise of two hemispheres.